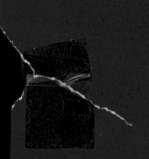

T0285205

FUTURES OF THE ARCHITECTURAL EXHIBITION

Mario Ballesteros, Giovanna Borasi, Ann Lui, Ana Miljački, Zoë Ryan, Martino Stierli, Shirley Surya

in Conversation with Students

Edited by Reto Geiser
and Michael Kubo

PARK BOOKS

CONTENTS

RETO GEISER AND MICHAEL KUBO
Exhibitions as Discourse

Over the last fifty years, exhibitions have proven to be a vital medium for architectural discourse, serving as platforms through which institutions and audiences have attended to architecture's social, cultural, political, and environmental responsibilities.

GABRIELA DEGETAU, CLAIRE ELESTWANI, ANA ESCOBAR, DRAKE FLOOD, KOHEN HUDSON, SHREE KALE, JIAYE LI, NICOLE LIDE, MITCH MACKOWIAK, JACK MURPHY, AYLIN NAZLI, IRENE NGUYEN, KAEDE POLKINGHORNE, MATTHEW RAGAZZO, SHEILA RODRIGUEZ, SAMANTHA SCHUERMANN, ESTHER TANG, SONIA TORRALBA, NYX VALERDY, JANE VAN VELDEN, CLAIRE WAGNER, ASHLEY WHITESIDES, TIFFANY XU

Students from the Rice University School of Architecture and the Gerald D. Hines College of Architecture and Design at the University of Houston in conversation with:

FUTURES OF THE ARCHITECTURAL EXHIBITION

CONTENTS

MARTINO STIERLI
The Exhibition as Research

The ambition of every exhibition project is to speak in meaningful ways both to the moment in which it's produced and to the longer arc of history. As historians, we have an obligation to continuously question and revisit preconceived notions of how history has been written and to be aware of the ways in which it is socially constructed.

GIOVANNA BORASI
Museum Work and Museum Problems

Our core public still comprises architects, intellectuals, critics, policymakers, and people who work within the fields of architecture and urbanism. But we advocate for the idea that architecture should become a concern for people not explicitly involved with the discipline.

ANA MILJAČKI
Tending to Discourse

All types of broadcasts—including exhibitions—have a place in these constellations of political issues, but for the Critical Broadcasting

Lab, exhibitions are also tools by which to probe, represent, and mirror specific topics or circumstances so they can be further discussed and understood.

ANN LUI
Curating Collective Space

279–315   We've seen so many examples of the ways in which institutions, because of old habits, fail their own purported values. I believe there has to be a way for institutions and individuals to be self-reflective and self-critical, and that doing so always makes the world around us richer, more interesting, and more expansive.

317–336   Appendix

RETO GEISER MICHAEL KUBO

EXHIBITIONS AS DISCOURSE

RETO GEISER AND MICHAEL KUBO

Over the last fifty years, exhibitions have proven
to be a vital medium for architectural discourse,
serving as platforms through which institutions
and audiences have attended to architecture's social,
cultural, political, and environmental responsibilities. With the notable exception of the Museum
of Modern Art (MoMA) in New York, which founded
its pioneering architecture and design department
in 1932, exhibition venues and museum collections
dedicated to architecture became widely established
in North America and Europe only after the end of
the 1970s. The Smithsonian Institution's National
Museum of Design (today the Cooper Hewitt) opened
in New York in 1976, followed by the Department
of Architecture and Design at the Art Institute of
Chicago (AIC) and the Venice Architecture Biennale
in 1980, the Deutsches Architekturmuseum in
Berlin in 1984, the Canadian Centre for Architecture (CCA) in Montreal in 1989, the architecture
collection of the Centre Pompidou in Paris in 1992,
and the Netherlands Architecture Institute in
Rotterdam in 1993. This network of institutions grew
in parallel with a range of private galleries that
opened in these years, such as Aedes Architecture
Forum in Berlin in 1980, or that began exhibiting
architecture to cater to a growing market for
architectural media, including the Drawing Center

and Leo Castelli Gallery (both after 1977) and Max Protetch Gallery (after 1979) in New York.[1] In the decades since, this exhibitionary complex has served as a primary site for architectural thinking and production within the design professions and as a key interface for shaping awareness of and interest in architecture for nondisciplinary audiences.

In recent years, numerous curators have explored new approaches that challenge traditional understandings of how architecture should be displayed, seeking to reframe the space of the architectural exhibition as a means for staging and discussing matters of both public and disciplinary concern in relation to the built environment. Across a wide range of venues—from small-scale, pop-up spaces and temporary sites to meta-exhibitions, events, and spectacles in the form of biennials and triennials, to more stable institutional spaces and their related collections and archives—these practitioners have expanded the scope of the architectural exhibition to encompass new formats for public debate, knowledge production, and even action. Such shifts have come as the design disciplines undergo a profound reckoning with architecture's ongoing complicity in structural forms of racism and exclusion and the ongoing impacts of historical processes of spatial violence on contemporary conditions. In this context, recent exhibitions speak to the charged questions of race, class, gender, labor, and identity that have accompanied architecture's stocktaking with regard to equity and social justice. In many cases, these exhibitions have sought to catalyze changes in how we understand and approach the spatial and environmental issues that are implicated in this realignment, from density to living standards, infrastructure, climate, and sustainability. Contemporary exhibitions have also speculated on the boundaries between architecture and other forms of spatial practice, the role of the architect in society, the conditions of architectural labor, and the means and methods of architectural production in relation to broader cultural and political concerns.

As the cultural stakes of the exhibition have changed, new curatorial approaches to the methods for displaying architecture have evolved in turn. The particularities of exhibiting architecture—as a body of techniques separate from other forms of exhibition-making and display in the arts—have also come under renewed scrutiny, both in the museum world and among independent curators. Architecture's presence in a gallery setting demands discipline-specific approaches to issues of content, audience, organization, narrative, and display, as well as to the institutional practices of collection and classification that underlie those issues. Despite such new approaches, the form and content of many recent architectural exhibitions suggest that both architectural and museological professionals continue to grapple with the central problem of how to represent external sites and objects within the extent of the gallery space, where those sites and objects are displaced in time, location, and use from their "real" presence in the outside world.[2] A further dilemma of curating architecture is that built work as such is necessarily impossible to include in collections and can be manifested in the gallery only via other forms of media, such as drawings, models, photographs, renderings, building materials, office documents, films, or publications. These challenges have prompted new curatorial responses to long-standing questions: How can the specificities of architectural space be experienced or made legible in the gallery setting? What strategies for representing architecture are appropriate for a broad public versus a discipline-specific audience? Is there a language of display that is specific to architectural exhibitions? How can exhibitions actively engage visitors with architectural ideas and concerns, and how can these be translated into cohesive sequences in space and time?

RETO GEISER AND MICHAEL KUBO

Futures of the Architectural Exhibition investigates the ways contemporary curators have approached these and other questions of display and the representation of space in specific exhibitions and in their stewardship of diverse institutional platforms for the representation of architecture and design, from major international museums to small galleries, informal venues, and academic research collaboratives. This small volume records a series of conversations on the future of architectural exhibitions, conducted from 2018 to 2021 with seven curators who were invited to give public lectures and lead student workshops at Rice University, the University of Houston, the Moody Center for the Arts, and the Glassell School of Art at the Museum of Fine Arts, Houston: Mario Ballesteros (Archivo Diseño y Arquitectura, Mexico City), Giovanna Borasi (CCA, Montreal), Ann Lui (Night Gallery, Chicago, and U.S. Pavilion, Venice Biennale), Ana Miljački (Critical Broadcasting Lab, Massachusetts Institute of Technology), Zoë Ryan (AIC and the Institute of Contemporary Art, University of Pennsylvania), Martino Stierli (The Museum of Modern Art, New York), and Shirley Surya (M+, Hong Kong). This project began as a joint masterclass held in the fall of 2018 at Rice University and the University of Houston in which international

curators from the United States, Mexico, and
Canada presented their work and led workshops
in conversation with students. Following public
lectures by these invited guests and responses from
local historians and curators, we then engaged our
visitors in an extended critical discussion of their
institutional approaches to the representation of
space through the techniques and formats of the
architectural exhibition. The mixture of institutions and voices allowed for the construction of a
sophisticated view of architectural curation, one
that uses the history of architectural exhibitions as
a reference point for studying the changing disciplinary definitions and roles of research, criticism,
and curating. The conversations also examined the
historical, political, and institutional conditions
under which specific exhibitions were conceived
and mounted, their contributions to seminal disciplinary conversations, and their critical reception.
In spring 2019 we continued the exploration of the
architectural exhibition through "Exhibiting Space,"
a co-taught seminar on the history of significant
exhibitions of architecture and design over the
last century. Our work continued with additional
dialogues conducted virtually through early 2021,
many including the same students who had participated in the earlier masterclass and seminar.

RETO GEISER AND MICHAEL KUBO

The nature of these conversations has evolved considerably in the four years since we initiated *Futures of the Architectural Exhibition*, mirroring profound cultural and political shifts in the contemporary world. Inspired by ever-more present struggles to achieve greater forms of social and environmental justice in the built environment, we increasingly felt the need to expand the voices and venues present in these dialogues to keep pace with the changing urgencies to which curators and institutions are responding. We also sought to address some of our own blind spots, such as our initial focus on institutionally affiliated curators who could speak critically to museological issues of collecting and display—rather than, for example, the contemporary context of biennials and triennials as venues for architectural discourse. We complemented these voices with those of curators who act through more itinerant or external relationships to conventional structures. Two-plus years of a global pandemic also inevitably shifted our thinking, prompting new questions about the continuing and future relevance—or not—of physical space for displaying and discussing architecture and the challenges of appropriating the digital realm for similar or new-but-related purposes. More pragmatically, the virtual also allowed us to expand our geographical and institutional scope beyond the initial, in-person constraints of the project to encompass conversations beyond the North American curatorial context. We also worked with the invited curators and students to revisit our earliest conversations as the project developed, offering opportunities to expand on their themes in response to current events. For all of these reasons, the transcripts presented here are not merely unedited recordings of our discussions as they originally took place but are the end results of a continuous process of editing, clarification, and revision. To give primacy to the curators' words and avoid unnecessarily complicating the discussions, the multiple discussants who also participated in these conversations, including students and invited faculty, have been condensed in each case to a single voice.

The edited dialogues, collected as *Futures of the Architectural Exhibition*, offer seven approaches to exhibiting architecture and collectively form a critical contribution to current discussions in art and architecture about curatorial practice and the techniques and formats of exhibiting architectural space. Through the positions presented in this book, we argue that architectural exhibitions constitute a key form of projection for both research and criticism in architecture and design and thus a discrete mode for producing reflections on the conditions of contemporary life through the built environment. Beyond the projection of built and unbuilt architectural works into the space of the gallery, and the exhibition of projects and forms of representation based on projective drawing, such as architectural perspectives and renderings, the conversations assembled here encompass the projection of possible futures for public life and urban space through the communicative medium of the exhibition.

In "Shaping Positions," Zoë Ryan explores the impact of architecture and design exhibitions on society through her work as chief curator at the AIC and through her book *As Seen: Exhibitions That Made Architecture and Design History*, the first publication to explore in depth the important role that exhibitions have played in the history of design practice. Ryan discusses the responsibility of museums to educate a broad public about the theoretical and ideological underpinnings of architecture, underscoring the importance of audience in the process of conceiving the display of works. She argues that exhibitions should set a stage to reframe our understanding of the world through architectural and design ideas that pose critical questions for the audience.

INTRODUCTION

Mario Ballesteros outlines the pragmatic, do-it-yourself approach to research and exhibition-making he developed at Archivo Diseño y Arquitectura in Mexico City. An object archive and exhibition space that opened to the public in 2012 and closed its doors permanently in 2019, Archivo was the only nonprofit institution in Mexico dedicated to collecting, exhibiting, and rethinking architecture and design. In "Exposing the Margins," Ballesteros advocates for the construction of images through architecture and the need to collect and integrate anonymous objects that do not have an archival history alongside more conventionally "authored" or canonical objects. As a counterpart to its nimble exhibition practices, Archivo's website is conceived as an alternative curatorial space that allows for the organization's exhibitions to transgress the limits of its physical space.

In the conversation "Curating as Collection-Building," Shirley Surya, the architecture curator of M+ in Hong Kong, reflects on this new museum's unique position and its remit to collect design and architecture in addition to visual art and the moving image. Surya discusses the interdisciplinary nature of the museum and how it informs the organization's approach to collecting, which is driven not only by cultural and regional concerns but also by an interest in objects that present parallels, affinities, or similar patterns of production. She addresses how bringing together both the canonical and the noncanonical can create an expanded discourse to engage audiences from the scholarly to the wider public. Finally, to bridge physical space and the virtual realm, Surya introduces approaches to online exhibitions and discusses the challenges of digital media.

In "The Exhibition as Research," Martino Stierli introduces the current trajectory and possible futures of architectural exhibitions at The Museum of Modern Art in New York. Stierli elaborates on the challenge of architectural display and its necessity to convey a broader context through proxies such as drawings, photographs, and fragments. He reflects on the increasingly social, contextual approach to exhibitions, including the trend of focusing on movements, geographies, or historical periods that have historically been underrepresented, marginalized, and less visible. A scholar and curator, Stierli stresses the importance of exhibition-making as a collaborative research practice, and he encourages efforts to capture as broad an audience as possible, including through the medium of the exhibition catalog, which he understands as an extension of the museum.

INTRODUCTION

Giovanna Borasi describes "Museum Work and Museum Problems" through the lens of her directorship of the CCA, which in recent years has produced exhibitions that explore alternative ways of practicing and evaluating architecture and give particular attention to the ways in which environmental, political, and social issues influence the contemporary built environment. Borasi talks about the importance of reaching a broader audience through more immersive experiences. As the director of a research institution with a significant archive, Borasi points to the importance and challenges of collecting and exhibiting digital artifacts and the new research questions they open, as well as the importance of building a global community to expand the CCA's role from a collecting institution to an instigator of research on overlooked areas.

In "Tending to Discourse," Ana Miljački presents her work as founding director of the Critical Broadcasting Lab at the Massachusetts Institute of Technology, a platform for discursive interventions in architecture culture whose key medium is the architectural exhibition, broadened to include experiments within the contemporary ecology of broadcast media. The Lab focuses on producing statements, artifacts, broadcasts, and interventions into architectural discourse. Miljački argues that the exhibition is a political outpost and that curatorial thinking can allow students to produce in modalities beyond professional design, experiences that will serve them as both architects and citizens by connecting discourse to political agency. Moving away from understanding architecture as an isolated object, Miljački's Lab expands the disciplinary discourse to include issues of labor, bureaucracy, and intellectual property.

Ann Lui, in "Curating Collective Space," reflects on exhibitions as places to do and share work while negotiating among multiple voices and stakeholders. Lui acknowledges the tension between valuing disciplinary expertise and expanding the boundaries of the discipline; that is, between depth of knowledge and breadth of experimentation. Bridging international exhibitions such as the U.S. Pavilion in Venice and community-focused venues such as Chicago's Night Gallery, Lui argues that architects should think about how to share a way of seeing and understanding buildings that leaves room for people to surprise us and to include narratives and perspectives that are not typically considered. A practitioner and curator, she advocates for an expansion of the exhibition's afterlife and reach through research, digital platforms, and publishing.

INTRODUCTION

This volume joins a group of recent book-length publications that have aimed to foreground the role of exhibitions in architectural discourse and to identify a variety of approaches to the unique challenges of curating architecture. These have included efforts to identify a canon of significant architecture and design exhibitions over the last century and to document in more detail the histories of individual exhibitions within this emerging canon, some through interviews with their curators.[3] Other recent publications have sought to develop theoretical categories or labels in order to chart a wide spectrum of contemporary positions on curating architecture and design.[4] In contrast, *Futures of the Architectural Exhibition* emphasizes the working dilemmas and opportunities faced by practicing curators in the current moment. The aim is not to create a comprehensive map of the field but to offer multiple perspectives that point toward possible directions for architectural exhibitions in the years to come. As such, the conversations in this book foreground what is present and what is projective in the curators' responses to the contemporary issues of representation and political agency and how those issues have been reflected in the changing context of the architectural exhibition. The conversations included here are neither exclusively insider discussions among curators nor academic conversations with historians or theorists. Rather, they are dialogues informed by the concerns of architecture students, for whom exhibitions are meaningful both as venues for disciplinary discourse and as possible sites of future work. The curators who participated in these conversations responded to students' questions about not only the definitions of architecture as reflected in the content of exhibitions but also more pragmatic issues of design, sequence, rhythm, media, audience, and attention as these are manifested in specific forms of display.

Futures of the Architectural Exhibition adds to the growing field of publications on architectural exhibitions by giving voice to the interests, positions, and imperatives of contemporary curators of architecture and design who represent a broad range of institutional and cultural contexts. In contrast to existing publications that focus on how specific exhibitions have affected architectural discourse or on architects and designers who have produced exhibitions as extensions of their practice, this book centers on the figure of the architectural curator, a distinct disciplinary figure representing multiple institutional perspectives on and approaches to exhibiting architecture. The seven curatorial positions highlighted in this publication reflect the specific challenges of operating within distinct institutional and noninstitutional settings and their differing frameworks for research, display, and engagement with both public and professional audiences. Reflecting shifts in contemporary curatorial thinking in response to a changing present, these dialogues suggest pathways toward multiple possible futures for the architectural exhibition.

1   On the origins and history of this network of galleries, collectors, and institutions after 1970, see Jordan Kauffman, *Drawing on Architecture: The Object of Lines, 1970–1990* (Cambridge, MA: MIT Press, 2018).
2   See Eeva-Liisa Pelkonen with Carson Chan and David Andrew Tasman, *Exhibiting Architecture—A Paradox?* (New Haven: Yale School of Architecture, 2015).
3   These include Zoë Ryan, ed., *As Seen: Exhibitions That Made Architecture and Design History* (Chicago: Art Institute of Chicago; New Haven: Yale University Press, 2017); Léa-Catherine Szacka, *Exhibiting the Postmodern: The 1980 Venice Architecture Biennale* (Milan: Marsilio, 2016); Eeva-Liisa Pelkonen, *Exhibit A: Exhibitions That Transformed Architecture, 1948–2000* (New York: Phaidon, 2018); and Szacka, *Biennials/Triennials: Conversations on the Geography of Itinerant Display* (New York: Columbia Books on Architecture and the City, 2019).
4   These include Cynthia Davidson, ed., "Curating Architecture," special edition, *Log 20* (Fall 2010); and Fleur Watson, *The New Curator: Exhibiting Architecture and Design* (Abingdon, UK: Routledge, 2021).

ZOË RYAN

SHAPING POSITIONS

ZOË RYAN

What is your role as a curator in broad-casting architecture and design culture to nondisciplinary audiences? How has that role related to the institutional missions of the Art Institute of Chicago, where you were chair and curator of architecture and design from 2011 to 2020, and in your current position at the Institute of Contemporary Art in Philadelphia?

I've worked in a range of institutions from small to large, some with a more disciplinary focus, others spanning thousands of years of creative practice. I've always seen my role as being a cheerleader for architects, designers, and artists and a champion and supporter of their projects. My role has been to ensure that architecture and design are seen as being as important as any other creative practice and as significant portals for the imagination.

The Art Institute was often the first place where disadvantaged young people could experience art, as it had been so stripped from public school education in Chicago. As an institution committed to inspiring an interest in art and culture and supporting audiences in their explorations of art as part of their studies and life, the museum's role was extremely important. In addition, as one of the birthplaces of modern architecture, Chicago was ripe for recontextualizing and rethinking architecture and design in our time. Everyone is an architecture critic in that town, building on their own understanding and reading of the built environment through personal experience. It was an incredible starting point for our department's work.

The Institute of Contemporary Art (ICA) at the University of Pennsylvania in Philadelphia was founded in 1963 by the dean of the School of Architecture, G. Holmes Perkins. From the beginning, the institution had an interdisciplinary focus, and I'm interested in helping shape that and furthering the ICA's role as an incubator of ideas and a forum for bringing people together to share in conversations around art and society.

Museums are in a challenging place right now. If elementary schools are no longer going to provide arts education then the museum's responsibility is much greater, because we become the point of entry for many people. What are you learning from being at the museum? Do we have a responsibility to educate people about architecture? While I don't think it's for me to teach people, I do feel a responsibility to help people gain a better understanding of architecture and design and to ensure that the two disciplines have a secure place at the table alongside other artistic practices. Particularly architecture. The stakes are so high that those conversations should be robust. Of course, responsibility for better educating the public about architecture might then shift. Architecture is about ideas and theoretical concepts, not just the nuts and bolts of constructing, though sometimes we do get to talk about that too.

> In your book *As Seen: Exhibitions That Made Architecture and Design History* (2017), you describe exhibitions curated by architects, magazine editors, or other disciplinary characters, such as *This Is Tomorrow* (1956), curated by *Architectural Design* editor Theo Crosby, and *MAN transFORMS* (1976), curated by architect Hans Hollein. What is your opinion of architects or other professional "outsiders" operating as curators in a museum setting?

What was so fascinating to me about working on that book was coming to the realization that, within architecture and design, exhibitions have been critical to advancing ideas. ○   It's impossible to gain a thorough understanding of these fields without evaluating exhibitions. What's interesting is

○
Zoë Ryan, ed., *As Seen: Exhibitions That Made Architecture and Design History* (Chicago: Art Institute of Chicago; New Haven: Yale University Press, 2017).

that exhibitions of architecture and design throughout the twentieth century and continuing into the
twenty-first century have been created by a range
of professionals, including curators, critics, and
practicing designers and architects, attesting to the
multifarious voices that have shaped these fields.
The field of curating architecture and design is
relatively new. To date, the Venice Architecture
Biennale, for example, has been curated predominantly by architects. When I studied art history,
there weren't as many design or architecture history
programs and few curatorial programs. Today,
however, there are many more, including specialized
courses related to curating architecture and design,
which could potentially shift thinking and practice.
The Critical, Curatorial, and Conceptual Practices
program at Columbia University's Graduate
School of Architecture, Planning and Preservation
is a good example of a course that is widening
the conversation.

What's challenging is that architects constantly have to present and interpret their own
work. They have to push it out there and articulate
it, justify it, emphasize it. It's inherent to the pro-
fession. This is why making exhibitions becomes
complex when suddenly there's a curator whose role
is to help interpret an architect's work. Architects

think they can do everything. As an architecture and design curator, you are collaborating with architects, but at a certain point you have to impose some critical distance if you're going to say what you need to about their work.

> In your talk in our Futures of the Architec-
> tural Exhibition lecture series, you described
> the formative experience of traveling with
> your mother to see art when you were
> young. Which exhibitions captured your
> attention, and why?

I remember visiting Barbara Hepworth's studio and home in St Ives in England. I loved seeing her work in the place where she made it and where she lived. That was a powerful experience. The show I remember most vividly as a student is *Sensation*, which was on view at the Royal Academy of Arts in London in 1997. The exhibition included works like Damien Hirst's *The Physical Impossibility of Death in the Mind of Someone Living* (1991), Sarah Lucas's *Au Naturel* (1994), and Chris Ofili's *The Holy Virgin Mary* (1996). You can imagine a young student seeing all of this and realizing, "This is art!" What stuck with me most was the possibility for art to reflect on society at a particular moment in time, as well as the potential for an exhibition to help launch the careers of a new generation of artists.

Until that point, I wasn't interested in contemporary art. I was more interested in historical art. I remember going to Madrid and being fascinated not only with Surrealism but also with the extraordinary realism of paintings by Rogier van der Weyden that I saw in the Museo del Prado, such as *The Descent from the Cross* (ca. 1435). I can still picture the tears, like glass marbles on the face of the Virgin.

> What do you see as the museum's roles and responsibilities in addressing contemporary social and political issues? Do design exhibitions offer a framework for reflection, or can they instigate forms of social change more directly?

My work is centered on exploring the social, political, and cultural implications of the arts. Architecture and design are inextricably linked to every aspect of our lives and are powerful tools for asking critical questions that open up new readings of the world. What I most appreciate about artistic practice is that it's conceptual—it's about ideas. It compels us to look closely and reflect on who we are and our relationships with the world and one another.

Curatorial practice is not one thing but can be many different types of practices and approaches. It has often been viewed very narrowly. I think our role as cultural producers is to study the art, the architecture, the design, but also to study the ideas of art, architecture, and design. For me this is critical. I'm interested in these artistic fields as ideological tools that can help frame and reframe our understanding of the world.

At the Art Institute, I took an issue-driven approach, developing projects around work that explored urgent concerns, whether the politics of health, reproductive rights, urban development, climate change, or beauty. I see my role within institutions as creating projects that position pressing issues and questions that help us shape a more just society, now more urgently than ever. Recently on view at the Art Institute was a project I curated with Ambiguous Standards Institute (ASI). Based in Istanbul, ASI is a research-based collective that investigates how standards develop—whether for time, measurements, building components, food, or healthcare—and assesses their impact on daily life. ○ Their research makes clear that although the world is becoming more standardized, ambiguous standards (or the lack of standards) are equally pervasive. The exhibition and the collective's online

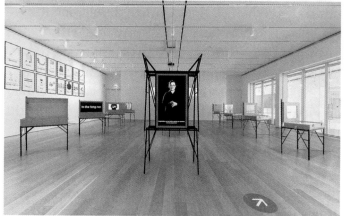

○
Ambiguous Standards Institute, *Ambiguous Standards of Food: Eggs and Holders*, 2021 (top).
Ambiguous Standards Institute: An Institute within an Institute, Exhibition at the Art Institute of Chicago, 2021 (bottom).
Images courtesy of Ambiguous Standards Institute.

archive invite us to consider the implications and shortcomings of a standardized world that profoundly shapes our lived experiences. At a time when standards of health and access to information and resources are being rethought across the globe in light of the COVID-19 pandemic and the movement for social and racial justice, ASI's research takes on new urgency.

> What tools can curators use to develop more inclusive representations of architecture and design, particularly representations that center historically marginalized voices?

As cultural workers, we need to take accountability for our work. I think exhibitions are a way to shine a light both on our own institutions and on overlooked narratives, places, and figures that are deserving of further exploration. I've spent my career supporting underrecognized talent and positioning alternative narratives from across cultures, geographies, and disciplines as a way to rethink the canon. I don't think it's about discarding existing narratives but offering alternative perspectives, adding to the canon, being honest about how the museum has been formulated, the types of collections it has and doesn't have. For example, at the Art Institute, we increasingly diversified our program and the types of work we exhibited and collected at the museum in an effort to broaden the conversation. We worked hard to find, collect, and exhibit work by women such as Marion Mahony Griffin, Charlotte Perriand, Tatiana Bilbao, Amanda Williams, Hella Jongerius, Reiko Sudo, and Christien Meindertsma. We were also building a collection of work by African American designers, especially those who had or were making their mark in Chicago; for example, designers such as Charles Harrison, a long-time teacher at the School of the Art Institute in Chicago, who developed the first plastic trash can and reinvented everyday objects such as toasters, sewing machines, and children's toys like the View-Master. More recently we acquired the *Sinmi Stool* (2012) by Norman Teague, who drew inspiration from beyond the Western canon of design and from art and music. The design of the *Sinmi Stool* reflects Teague's self-identification as an African American designer with a personal connection to the Yoruba language. ○

The ICA shares these values. It has long championed diverse voices and projects that help audiences grapple with and make sense of the world. Experimentation and risk-taking are part

○
Norman Teague, *Sinmi Stool* (2015, prototype/2020, limited edition).
Photograph by Jonathan Allen.
Image courtesy of Norman Teague.

of the ICA's DNA. We continue to reach beyond the canon while redefining it. I'm keenly interested in the ways ICA can continue to foster individual and collective agency by developing projects that reflect on and challenge our lived experiences. Coming from architecture and design, I'm interested in the potential to collectively and creatively redesign the institution from the inside out, prioritizing access, equity, and multivocality in all of our work—from how we develop the organization's culture behind the scenes to how we design our programs, how we identify and animate issues we want to address through visitor-centric experiences both online and offline, how we contribute to our community, both local and international, and how we bring audiences into our work as valuable partners. Even to how we animate the spaces of ICA's building, an issue that has been critical during the COVID-19 pandemic.

How does collaboration figure into this approach?

When I joined the Art Institute, I came from a small nonprofit organization, the Van Alen Institute in New York, whose mission is to improve the design of the public realm. It's small but feisty. Collaboration across institutions and areas of expertise is an inherent part of the organization. Similarly, I see my work at the ICA as increasingly being about collaboration and working with others within and outside the organization to build projects that are more multidimensional. My curatorial projects have always relied on collaboration and input from other sources to help steer ideas and shape the project. It's important to acknowledge this and make these connections visible. I couldn't have done an exhibition like *In a Cloud, in a Wall, in a Chair: Six Modernists in Mexico at Midcentury*, which opened at the Art Institute in 2019, without a vast network of collaborators and experts. I don't think you ever begin a project knowing all the answers, but you do need to be sure you have a concept strong enough to drive a thought-provoking investigation. Then you can identify the questions that need answering and engage in meaningful ways with the experts who are equipped to answer those questions with you. I really enjoy working this way and bringing people together.

> Which curatorial projects have been partic-
> ularly effective in framing these narratives
> for audiences?

With the *In a Cloud* exhibition, we thought a lot
about how and for whom we were framing the
conversation around the exhibition. ○   It was
a multilayered and complex project that looked
beyond the idea of the solo genius and brought
together networks of knowledge and connections
around six artists and designers: Clara Porset, Lola
Álvarez Bravo, Anni Albers, Ruth Asawa, Cynthia
Sargent, and Sheila Hicks. Our hope was to set
the record straight, to make Mexico better known
as a site of modern art and design and to highlight
six figures who all benefitted from and contributed
to Mexico's artistic landscape from the 1940s to
the 1970s. It was a story about the complexities
of cross-cultural exchange. The exhibition invited
audiences to interrogate the gaps and ask questions
about who benefits from and who has the power in
these processes. It was also a show about migration.
It was a reminder that, for many people, transnational migration is both a fact of life and a provo-
cation to creativity. The exhibition challenged easy
assumptions about the directions that migration
can take. Current political discourse in the United

FRAMING THE CONVERSATION

○
Installation view of the exhibition *In a Cloud, in a Wall, in a Chair: Six Modernists in Mexico at Midcentury*, September 6, 2019 to January 12, 2020, Galleries 182–184, The Art Institute of Chicago.
Image courtesy of the Art Institute of Chicago.

ZOË RYAN

States doesn't often frame Mexico as a destination for migration. As this exhibition made clear, however, Mexico's openness to artistic practice drew a host of ambitious modern artists and designers from around the world. These issues resonate today as much as they did at midcentury.

> Both public opinion and architectural criticism can impact how an exhibition is received and how it reverberates after its closure. How do you navigate the expectations of audiences?

Making exhibitions is all about creating juxtapositions. If you have three things next to one another, they will inevitably be in conversation with each other. Our job is to set up those interesting visual and physical juxtapositions so that audiences can make their own connections and interpret the works for themselves. Creating multiple entry points for visitors is essential. We're always looking for ways to create a range of interpretive tools, from wall labels to how we design exhibition displays, to digital tools that help visitors inform their own readings of the work, whether they're experts in the field or not. I think it's incredibly important to center the audience when making work, to hear from them, and to determine outcomes based on their experience and input. Every project is an opportunity to test different strategies of engagement and find ways to support audiences in recognizing their own capacity to be imaginative thinkers and producers of knowledge.

In my last few years in Chicago, I taught a class at the School of the Art Institute on the history of architecture and design exhibitions. I learned a lot from working with the students, who were all extremely engaged and interested in issues related to institutional methods of display. I invited my colleague Emily Fry, the Art Institute's head of interpretation, to lead one of the classes, which was extremely eye-opening for me. The students gave feedback on our new installation of modern and contemporary architecture and design. Based on their feedback on wall labels, placement of texts, and types of objects and narratives on display, I was able to see my own blind spots and find ways to think through them, to improve the stories we were telling and why, and to identify gaps and holes to fill, which we began to work on. We also rewrote some wall texts and changed the placement of other texts, including moving the introductory panel so that it was positioned in a more comfortable part of the gallery for viewers to read. This type of feedback is essential and important to learn from.

> What other methods do curators have to capture the attention of a diverse audience and encourage different forms of engagement?

I really enjoy working with teens, who are incredibly quick, insightful, and unafraid to tell you what they think. In an exhibition, they pan the room, see everything you're trying to do, and judge whether it's a success. If we manage to engage teens in an exhibition, then I think it's a success. When we use multidisciplinary terminology, we should explain what it means or we shouldn't use it at all. Let's speak clearly.

Younger age groups also often gravitate to the moving image as a starting point for learning about an object, an exhibition, a time period, and so on. Through those more accessible entry points, they then tackle other areas. At the Art Institute, the architecture and design team was inspired to explore film as a forum for storytelling. Curator Alison Fisher spearheaded the making of a series of films on important works for the modern and contemporary architecture and design galleries, including a prefabricated bathroom and kitchen from Les Arcs, a ski resort that designer Charlotte Perriand masterminded in the 1970s (it still exists today). ○ Alison went with a film crew to the ski chalet in France. She also included field interviews with experts who spoke about Perriand's project in more detail. The film, still on display next to the prefabricated bathroom and kitchen units, helps bring those pieces to life and illustrates how they functioned in their original location. We also chose not to rebuild the units in a pristine way in the gallery. We displayed them in their raw state, with the piping exposed, the fiberglass and construction marks still visible. We felt this unfinished quality was important for people to understand what prefabrication is, how units arrive on site, and how they get locked into place.

I'm interested in continuing these discussions at ICA and learning from audiences in Philadelphia. In response to the pandemic and to encourage access to our programming from home, ICA recently launched virtual tours for all of our exhibitions. We are exploring ways to embed video, links to music, voice-overs, and narration as ways to animate these tours and give viewers a unique experience that complements seeing the works in the gallery. During the pandemic we pivoted all

ZOË RYAN

○
Charlotte Perriand, Prefabricated Kitchen Unit, Les Tournavelles, Arc
1800, Savoie, France, 1975–1978, 2014.1179, The Art Institute of Chicago.
Image courtesy of the Art Institute of Chicago.

of our public programming online, where it has drawn a robust international audience in addition to a vibrant local scene. Finding ways to connect with both is important as we continue to develop and experiment with how to create experiences in the gallery as well as in digital space.

> Speaking of moving images, to what degree do you think other contemporary media technologies, like visitors' personal devices, can be incorporated into the logic of exhibitions to create engagement?

For the *In a Cloud* exhibition, we developed an audio tour that visitors could download through an app on their phone. The curatorial team selected a few key works for audiences to have as a starting point for engaging with the material on view. We recorded comments from scholars, the curatorial team, and the artists whose work was on view, and we added additional information to the wall labels. At the ICA, we're exploring similar ideas to help tailor and enhance the visitor experience—whether in the space, on the go, or from home. There's a lot of potential for the development and expansion of ideas and conversations.

Then again, we can still achieve a lot with relatively lo-fi techniques. *In a Cloud* dealt with an important exhibition that took place in Mexico in 1952, curated by Clara Porset, that put craft and design on the same level for the first time, in very modernist displays. It looked much like MoMA's *Good Design* shows of the same era. It also had an amazing catalog, which is extremely difficult to get now. The Art Institute had a copy in their library, so we made a digital book that allowed visitors to flick through the pages themselves. We put it online and thus increased its circulation, restoring a difficult-to-find exhibition to the narrative of exhibition history.

EXHIBITION DESIGN

How do these concerns about audience and engagement impact your choices concerning the layout and organization of an exhibition as a sequence in plan?

The choreography of an exhibition is essential to how visitors experience and determine their own paths. It's important to create a legible system that's flexible enough to allow visitors to work within it, to make their own path, while still helping them understand the exhibition as a set of ideas that unfold spatially. I've always worked closely with architects and designers on the exhibition design to ensure that it reflects and reinforces the themes and ideas within the exhibition. For me, the exhibition design, the catalog, the public programs, and so on, are all essential components of a project and provide different ways of engaging and interpreting it for yourself.

How does the content and reception of an exhibition change through multiple iterations in different times or locations? For example, how did you translate the informal and ephemeral aspects of the second Istanbul Biennial, which you curated in 2014, into your subsequent exhibition

○
Installation view of the exhibition *The Future Is Not What It Used to Be*,
2nd Istanbul Design Biennial, 2014.
Image courtesy of Istanbul Foundation for Culture and Arts (IKSV).

of this material at the Art Institute in the exhibition *As Seen: Exhibitions That Made Architecture and Design History* (2015)?

As part of the Istanbul Design Biennial, we curated a brief history of architecture and design exhibitions from 1956 to 2006. ○ These ranged from the 1956 Whitechapel Gallery exhibition *This Is Tomorrow* to Expo '70 in Osaka to *Massive Change* at the Vancouver Art Gallery in 2005. It was a way to position the Istanbul Biennial as part of a continuum of projects and emphasize the influence of exhibitions in the field and how they have framed ideas. The initial display was created as a lo-fi presentation of materials from exhibitions with texts on the show, catalogs, and in some cases films to show how these projects were realized. We had such tremendous feedback on this research that we decided to develop it further. At the Art Institute, we built on the project, making the texts more pointed in articulating how each exhibition had presented an idea. We added more material, much of it sourced online, such as brochures and invite cards. And we added more installation photos, blown up as large-scale wallpapers, to help visitors get a better sense of the exhibitions. Following the exhibition and more great feedback from visitors and peers, we decided to take the research and develop it into a book, *As Seen*. The book looks at eleven case studies across fifty years and gathers materials and essays on each exhibition. We realized that few books documented or discussed architecture and design exhibitions and their history, so the project seemed like a necessary contribution to the field. In our case, the exhibitions became the source material for the book.

As an aside, sometimes I wonder how we were able to make *The Future Is Not What It Used to Be*, the project for the Istanbul Design Biennial. ○   I had never curated a biennial before, and I could never have done the show in Istanbul the way I would do it at the Art Institute. In Istanbul we threw the exhibition together; it was scrappy, but that's also what I loved about it. Our team conducted the research, but we were an international collective representing multiple disciplines and countries. At the time, Turkey was in serious social and political turmoil. The streets were alive. We had no idea what was happening. We didn't even know if the biennial was relevant or if we should be making exhibitions in such a moment. Because the exhibition could easily have been cut from Turkey's cultural programming, we kept coming back to how we could make sure the biennial would keep going.

○
The Future Is Not What It Used to Be, 2nd Istanbul Design Biennial,
Galata Greek Primary School, 2014 (top).
Image courtesy of Istanbul Foundation for Culture and Arts (IKSV).
Installation view of the exhibition *As Seen: Exhibitions That Made
Architecture and Design History*, October 1, 2015 to August 14, 2016,
Gallery 286, The Art Institute of Chicago (bottom).
Image courtesy of the Art Institute of Chicago.

> How do you translate these exhibition
> strategies into publications that can have a
> longer life span or instigate different forms
> of engagement?

Books are such a privilege to work on. I say "books" specifically because I'm not really interested in creating exhibition catalogs as such. The book should be its own thing. It's an opportunity to build on the content of the show and reflect on it. For me, work on a book often happens far in advance of the exhibition. The thesis of the show gets honed and fine-tuned as I'm writing my essay, and the checklist for the exhibition adapts accordingly. You can say so much more in a book to contextualize the projects on display, but nothing beats seeing the works for oneself.

I think the same questions you ask yourself with an exhibition have to be asked when making a book. You always have to focus on your audience. In the catalog, though, you can go into far more depth. I wouldn't say necessarily that my language or ideas are different in the book than in an exhibition, but they are more fleshed out. Usually, a host of other writers are also involved with a book. Of course, I don't tell them how to write, but you invite specific people to contribute to your vision. In the case of *As*

Seen, this was a series of focused looks at different approaches to exhibitions.

> In some cases the difference you suggest between a book and a catalog becomes critical. Perhaps the most famous example is the *Modern Architecture: International Exhibition* at the Museum of Modern Art in New York in 1932, where the catalog was quite different from the much better known book that was published in parallel with it, *The International Style* (1932).

The catalog for *This Is Tomorrow* (1956) is another amazing example. It includes plans of the gallery; it was envisioned as a guidebook (its small format and ring binding adds to this idea) that you bought before seeing the exhibition and then used as a guide to learn about the installations. At times the actual works from the show are depicted in the catalog; at other times there's a more theoretical exploration of the works on display, which reveals the different ways the exhibition was thought through by the participants. The book was envisioned as playing many roles at once. It wasn't a direct one-to-one of the show but was intended to develop the conversation around the exhibition. The book was also designed as an object in its own right. I strive to create these kinds of books.

There's a big distinction between a book and a catalog. As a document with an afterlife, it's gratifying when you can find a book that allows you to understand all of the works that were in an exhibition. But checklists often change. For me, the book can only ever be its own thing. It must be seen as something that lives on, that has a different life. Otherwise, you're dating it dramatically, because you're referring to something that happened, which is itself immediately out of date. So you try to give the book its own, lasting relevance.

SCALES OF ARCHITECTURE

Built works are often displayed in design
exhibitions through drawings, models, and
photographs. How do you gauge the ways
in which such representations show the
imagined versus the "real" building?

When an exhibition displays plans and drawings
exclusively, the viewer has to imagine what the
finished building might look like. That's not so easy.
Without photography, it can be difficult for people
to gauge whether a building was completed or is
just an idea. In 2011, Alison Fisher and I organized
the first comprehensive retrospective of architect
Bertrand Goldberg's work. ○   One of the questions we got repeatedly from visitors when we
gave tours was whether particular buildings had
been realized. The show had few photographs of
realized projects. We understood that this was a
critical oversight on our part. Many of the projects
had been realized; one could walk out of the show,
wander around Chicago, and see several of them.
That exhibition was our learning curve. A map of
where to find the works in the city would also have
been helpful.

Are there gaps between architecture's
disciplinary techniques and the built work

ZOË RYAN

○
Installation view of the exhibition *Bertrand Goldberg: Architecture of Invention*, September 7, 2011 to January 8, 2012, Galleries 283–285, The Art Institute of Chicago.
Image courtesy of the Art Institute of Chicago.

that can become productive in exhibitions;
for example, the fact that architects do
not directly make buildings but work
at a distance, producing instructions
and drawings?

We're always trying to articulate the main idea, to
convey what designers were trying to do. For the
Goldberg show, for example, we commissioned a
suite of models. They were all gray and composed
of simple volumes, so you could get a sense of
composition and key ideas. We did this purposely
so they could be distinguished from Goldberg's
built production. They were a didactic tool to help
visitors better understand the work and the show.
    That said, I don't focus on architects and
designers as problem solvers. They're really good at
asking questions and identifying key issues. Even
if we're talking about joints, curtain walls, and so
on, we have to come back to the fact that decisions
were made because of a thesis. In the best projects,
every decision is made because of a larger set of
issues and ideas. We do talk about compromises
and budget and all the other things architects and
designers have to address, but always in relation to
what they aimed to achieve, their vision. Take the
images of Ludwig Hilberseimer's urban plans, for

example. If we were living inside these images of pure isolation of the human, it would be horrific. Yet the drawings are absolutely amazing and have been so influential. Many positives came out of what he envisioned, ideas that have become part of the general discussion. We examine these ideas at their origin: Why were people thinking that way? What were they trying to say about the world? It's not that we're passing judgment, but we do want some level of critique.

> In several of your shows, such as *Making Place: The Architecture of David Adjaye* (2015), you've displayed fragments of a building within the exhibition space. How does the full-scale architectural fragment figure into your curatorial approach?

One of the interesting things about the Art Institute is that they've always collected parts of buildings. They have a reconstruction of the entire trading floor of the Chicago Stock Exchange, designed by Louis Sullivan, for example, including the ornamentation and wallpaper. One can stand within the room and feel as if someone is about to strike the gavel. The Art Institute is also known for its grand staircase, which has original fragments of buildings by Louis Sullivan and Frank Lloyd Wright, among many others, including large ornamental fragments such as stained-glass windows, screens, and gates. More recently the museum added to these narratives by including work from less well known architects such as Walter T. Bailey, the first licensed African American architect in Illinois. Each fragment and building part celebrates a specific site or place.

In our exhibition with David Adjaye, we were interested in how he roots his projects in place, memory, and material qualities. ○   He's intent on using architecture as a platform for opening up entrenched social rules and modes of human behavior for reexamination, as a way to provoke new thinking about the time and place in which we live and in which his projects are situated. Co-curator Okwui Enwezor and I were keen to include full-scale architectural elements in the exhibition as a way to punctuate the show, to create a sense of the formal and material qualities of his works and the ways David attaches these projects to a particular place. We also wanted to give audiences a firsthand and one-to-one-scale experience of David's architecture. We commissioned several large-scale fragments of parts of buildings at real scale and installed a full-scale pavilion, *Horizon*

Installation view of the exhibition *Making Place: The Architecture of David Adjaye*, September 16, 2015 to January 3, 2016, Galleries 283–285, 182–184, The Art Institute of Chicago.
Images courtesy of the Art Institute of Chicago.

(2007), which visitors could enter and experience. The large-scale pieces of important projects included the entry window to the Stephen Lawrence Centre (2007) with a window design by artist Chris Ofili, in memory of Lawrence, a black teenager murdered in London. We also installed a concrete cast of the facade of Sugar Hill (2014), a mixed-use building clad with rose-embossed, graphite-tinted precast panels, paying tribute to the rich culture and history of Harlem.

> The notion of futures appears in the titles of numerous shows you've curated, as well as in one of the key exhibitions in your *As Seen* book, *This Is Tomorrow* (1956). What role can exhibitions play in imagining possible futures?

I've always viewed exhibitions not as a means to an end or an end in themselves but as conversation starters. They're an occasion to explore the changing scope of artistic practice across fields and to emphasize the important role the arts play in identifying points of urgency and in posing questions. As critic and futurist Alvin Toffler forecast in 1970, what the world needs is a multiplicity of visions, dreams, and images of potential tomorrows. This idea seems as relevant today as it must have then. In our own time of rapid change and social and political struggle, it feels increasingly urgent to look at where we've come from, where we are, and where we're going. I've worked on two projects specifically focused on the future. Most recently, I was part of the curatorial team for *Designs for Different Futures* (Philadelphia Museum of Art, 2019; Walker Art Center, 2020–2021). The exhibition considered several possible futures through the lens of design. Grounded in real-life concerns, related to issues such as food production, gender identity, political agency, citizenship, and beauty, for example, the exhibition was presented as a handbook for future literacy. It explored projects from the conceptual to the practical that used future scenarios as foils to discuss and reshape our current lived experiences and, most important, to help our imaginations take flight.

The Istanbul Design Biennial in 2014 was another project that helped me understand design specifically as a field that is all about projecting forward, imagining new possibilities that can transform the present, and helping write new potential futures. Biennials by their nature are a litmus test of the state of society over a period of two years and have a long tradition of being focused on the future. Biennials, which often take place outside major art institutions, are valuable forums for bringing together a cross-section of ideas. They have the potential to highlight emerging voices from far-flung places and challenge dominant narratives through conversation and exchange, activities that are increasingly pertinent and necessary today. Working on the biennial, I kept returning to the words of Richard Hamilton, speaking about *This Is Tomorrow*, that they weren't intending to act as prophets—they felt that the only way to find out what might take place in the future was to look at what was going on in the present, to make the observer look more closely. I think this is exactly what exhibitions can do. They invite us to pause, focus our attention, and offer alternative perspectives and ideas that help inform new ways of seeing and thinking, so essential today. Borrowing from our title of the biennial, and thinking about the last, pandemic-filled year, if we've learned anything, it's that "the future is not what it used to be."

Zoë Ryan is the Daniel W. Dietrich, II Director of the Institute of Contemporary Art at the University of Pennsylvania. The initial conversation on which this text is based took place in Houston in August 2018, when she was the John H. Bryan Chair and Curator of Architecture and Design at the Art Institute of Chicago.

MARIO BALLESTEROS

EXPOSING THE MARGINS

MARIO BALLESTEROS

> What is your approach to curating
> exhibitions in the Mexican context? What
> is unique about Mexican architecture,
> particularly in terms of how images of
> this architecture have been constructed
> and presented in the past?

What's unique in the Mexican context is the effort
to project an image of a different type of modernity,
one that combines traditional and autochthonous
culture with the universality of the International
Style, or modernism. This effort started before the
Mexican Revolution, which lasted from 1910 to
1920, and was one of the earlier twentieth-century
social movements. It wasn't communist or socialist;
it was an agrarian, antidictatorial revolution.
The Eurocentric dictatorship of Porfirio Díaz pre-
tended to transition from an image of Mexico as
a backward, rural country toward one of a modern,
industrial nation. A good deal of this narrative
was constructed through architecture. There were
huge building projects, as in many other postcolonial or emerging economies of the time. The
government built ostentatious infrastructure
and public buildings with exquisite detailing as
symbolic representations of the state's power.
Díaz's slogan was *"Orden y progreso"* [order and

progress]. Building and architecture materialized this progress.

But even before the revolution and the flurry of architectural movements it generated, there was this question of what made Mexico different from other countries competing to be the most modern, most interesting, and most productive. From the late nineteenth century, Mexico relied on the national myth of pre-Hispanic greatness. The Mexican pavilion at the 1889 Exposition Universelle in Paris was dubbed the "Aztec palace." It was the weirdest building one could imagine, mixing neoclassical principles with reimagined pre-Columbian motifs.

How did Mexico's presence on the world stage—for example at the World's Fairs and other international exhibitions—further shape ideas of a Mexican architecture?

From the end of the nineteenth century through the 1960s, a clear and coherent thread ties together architecture, image, nationalism, and power as a result of modernization in Mexico. The government was physically constructing an image of Mexican culture through architecture.

The pavilion at the 1889 Exposition Universelle in Paris came at a moment when Mexico, as a nation, was starting to discover its "unique" or "deep" heritage—it was an age of exploration, and some of the first archaeological digs were getting underway in places like the Yucatán Peninsula. The pavilion spoke to an exoticism that was in vogue everywhere. ○   I think this process of self-exoticizing is tied to the building of national identity. The basic formula for defining modern Mexican culture was to blend the pre-Hispanic, the colonial, and the modern. Ideas of what was modern in the 1960s differed from those in the nineteenth century, but the formula stayed the same. In Mexico, unlike the United States, the big foundational myth was mixing: that we're a *mestizo* culture, a culture that's not segregated by race or ethnicity.

Something similar happened in architecture. Mexicans don't understand the modern as erasing the pre-Hispanic or the colonial but as a merging of ideas. Fernando Gamboa was a key figure in the construction of this image of Mexico through his exhibitions, painting, and writing. He wasn't an architect, but he curated every Mexican World's Fair pavilion from the 1930s to the 1970s. He called himself a museographer, but he was more a builder of national image through exhibitions. The formula of referencing pre-Hispanic motifs was repeated from the 1920s through the 1950s. You see it in the

Pavilion of Mexico, Paris Exposition (Exposition Universelle), Paris, France, 1889. Retrieved from the Library of Congress, https://www.loc.gov/item /91725830/.

Mexican pavilion, which won the gold medal at the 1958 Brussels World's Fair. Positioned at the entrance was an Aztec-inspired fountain dedicated to the oil economy; oil flowed out the top, a nod to when oil was nationalized and became part of the Mexican image.

The next significant moment in constructing a national image was in 1968, when the Olympics pushed Mexico City into the limelight, and a new version of the image and construction of "Mexicanness" emerged through architecture.

> Many architectural projects were commissioned during the years leading up to the 1968 Olympics. There seems to have been a concerted effort to transform the image of Mexico globally through Mexican art and architecture, as well as through the design elements of the Olympic Games itself.

More than new buildings, Mexico '68 was about graphics. These graphics bridged between Op Art, which was popular at the time, and vernacular references to Wixárika art and other Indigenous aesthetics. It was a foundational modern graphic exercise of an unprecedented scale for Mexico. The country didn't have resources to build new infrastructure for the Olympics, so it recycled most of its stadium infrastructure. With a limited budget, Pedro Ramirez Vázquez, who had been a co-architect of the Mexican Pavilion at the Brussels World's Fair, focused on temporary design interventions. He had a holistic and strategic view of design and was a believer in the philosophy of total design. He was the president of the organizing committee of the Olympics and brought together an incredible team. Eduardo Terrazas and Lance Wyman, a young American graphic designer, co-authored the whole Olympic identity. Vázquez really understood the soft power of design, which he executed through the simplest of gestures, like painting lampposts in different colors to function as waymarks to different sites. Because the Olympic venues were so spread out across the city, wayfinding became crucial for navigating from one venue to another. For the first time in the history of the Olympics, Mexico proposed a cultural Olympics. Mexico wasn't particularly good at sports. Culture, on the other hand, we had plenty of. Culture, and architecture and design as part of culture, has always been part of the official image of what Mexico is.

Can you discuss how Archivo's work engages with this complex history of architecture and exhibitions in Mexico, particularly in relation to the push for modernization and nation-building?

I think it's important for Archivo, as a contemporary space, to reflect on questions that have been persistent throughout the history of architecture and exhibitions in Mexico. Gamboa outlined these questions quite clearly: Are we traditional, or are we modern? Are we both? How does Mexico fit into the wider model of difference? We also have to understand that there were competing models in Gamboa's time of what was modern and how development was supposed to occur in the second half of the twentieth century. The Cold War drove different understandings of what modernization, internationalism, and culture were about. Mexico wasn't aligned with one side or the other but was trying to find the middle ground between these competing cultural and economic models. Positioning ourselves as non-aligned naturalized this tension between what's specific and what's universal about culture in Mexico. In that context Gamboa's formula of cultural *mestizaje* [crossbreeding], of reconciliation between Indigenous, colonial, and modern forces and principles was powerful and successful, but today it reads as an archaic distortion.

Archivo tries to pull apart this distortion and understand the bits and pieces behind the image.

Another important figure in exhibitions was Clara Porset, a Cuban émigré to Mexico in the late 1930s. She became the most important industrial, product, and furniture designer in Mexico. Porset is interesting because in the 1930s she went to Black Mountain College for a summer and became close with Josef and Anni Albers. Her life and work is a perfect example of direct links between Mexico and international modernism, be it through photography, architecture, art, or politics. Porset had been participating in shows at MoMA since the 1940s. If you look at her 1952 exhibition *Art in Daily Life: Well-Designed Objects Made in Mexico*, you see the connection to MoMA's *Good Design* exhibition held just two years prior. The links to what was going on elsewhere are clear-cut.

It's important to dig into the histories of these exhibitions, particularly ones that haven't survived as well-known architectural or design exhibitions, as a way of tracing changing ideas. But it's also important to dig into these histories to recognize ourselves in them. The same questions persist today about why Mexican architecture is important, interesting, or different, or what we as Mexican architects and designers push for. This is

similar to what was asked in previous decades, but
with a different purpose. Mexican architects don't
ask these questions today with the purpose of
selling an image but rather to try to sink their teeth
into them and to understand where previous gener-
ations went wrong.

THE COLLECTION

You've described Archivo as a space to discuss these difficult questions about Mexico's history. Archivo also uses its collection of objects to frame these questions. How is your curatorial approach to these subjects influenced by the status of particular kinds of objects, whether a mural, a coffeepot, or a Clara Porset chair? How do you recontextualize these objects to address these questions to a contemporary audience?

We have a challenging relationship with objects. Archivo's mission, when I began, was centered on the permanent collection. The setup of our first show was essentially a broomstick, a paper cup, and a Corona chair on a pedestal. Initially, curating the shows with these types of objects was fun, but after you do two or three similar shows the format gets tired. We really wanted to say that the objects in themselves are not the end but a means to push an idea. We want to say, "Yes objects are important, but not because of what they are, necessarily, but because of what they represent." For all of our shows we've made a conscious decision not to show beautiful objects with clear labels. In fact, we don't do labels at all. Instead,

MARIO BALLESTEROS

○
Installation view of the exhibitions *MXCD03* (top) and *MXCD01* (bottom),
Mexico Design City series, October 2016 and 2018, Archivo, Mexico City.
Photographs by Arturo Arrieta and Luis Young.
Images courtesy of Archivo.

we do beautiful poster handouts that function as maps of the exhibition space with text added.

Sometimes Archivo has received criticism that its shows are communicated as dealing with design holistically but that a given show doesn't feature graphic design, for instance. Our view has been that one show might push more into products, while another might push more into architecture, and so on. But then our critics respond that we're exhibiting not design but architecture—or worse, that we're doing art shows and not design at all. That's why I sometimes prefer the notion of material culture even more than design. ○ For me, *design* is already a generous, open term. I'm more interested in loose definitions than in strict categories.

Archivo has an archive of objects that make up the permanent collection. How is the current collection related to the personal collection of Fernando Romero, the founder of Archivo? Can you talk about Archivo's origins and about its acquisition of objects since then?

We have around two thousand objects in the permanent collection. The Archivo collection started as Fernando Romero's personal collection, which he began when he was still in architecture school. He's always been interested in architecture at different scales. He was drawn to the architectural logic of objects, and so he started collecting chairs. Soumaya Slim, Fernando's partner, also has an amazing fashion, accessory, textile, and shoe collection.

Fernando and Soumaya identified a void in Mexico: it doesn't have a dedicated design museum. Our "national architecture museum" is basically a hallway on the top floor of the Palacio de Bellas Artes, but there is no space dedicated to design. Mexican architecture schools don't have design or object collections either. UNAM, Mexico's premier research institution, doesn't even have an industrial design collection—they have a tiny student work collection. None of the existing institutions had shown much attention to Mexico's incredibly rich history of design. I think Fernando and Soumaya slowly started to realize that this was a void that Archivo, with its tiny scale and specific niche perspective, could fill.

Going back to the question of objects, what's interesting about material culture or the study of objects is that it allows a much more complex reading of history. It allows people, moments, or issues that wouldn't necessarily make it into the history books to be expressed. Kitchen appliances, for example, that would never be in a history book of the nineteenth or early twentieth century, are suddenly a lens for understanding specific histories from that period. We always try to read what's behind the object, including its social, political, cultural, and economic qualities.

Material culture is also relevant to understanding contemporary or recent history. For example, we've done a show on the history of video games—ones I played as a child. Video games as history sounds slightly ridiculous, and, as a result, the exhibition gains a certain tension. In general, we try not to fetishize objects or to focus only on beautiful examples of design—the amazing chairs or interiors—which is always a big risk when addressing design history.

MARIO BALLESTEROS

> As a director working in the current context
> of Archivo and wanting to rethink what's
> been previously done there, how do you
> balance Fernando's vision as the founder
> with your own vision for the collection?
> Are there challenges from within the insti-
> tution or outside pressures that you have
> to navigate?

We don't have any strictly commercial pressures. I'm
always amused when we think about Archivo as an
institution because we're so small—it's me negotiating with Fernando. We don't have a board, and we
don't respond to a large group of people or different
types of interests. This can be a huge advantage, but
it can also be difficult because the negotiation is
tight and specific. In general, the spirit of Archivo is
different from other institutional models. It's not a
display of an amazing personal collection of chairs.
Fernando is adamant about avoiding that model.
He prefers to be present, but Mexico has a different
culture regarding patronage than elsewhere.
Mexican institutions don't put people's names on
museum doors or toilets, for instance.

  When I came to Archivo, I didn't hire anyone for the first three months. All I received when
I arrived was a badly organized hard drive. During

those months, I was just one-on-one with Fernando, throwing out tons of ideas. I would suggest a show, and he would turn it down. Because of Fernando, I had to learn to understand the essence of a project and how to clearly communicate it in space. How could I communicate an ambitious show—like the *One Hundred Years in One Hundred Fragments* exhibition—in a simple sentence? ○   The sentence becomes, "The show is about understanding that design is not about the last twenty years; it's about the last one hundred years, and here are one hundred objects to show this history." The message becomes this simplified version, and, upon seeing the show, this world of objects and ideas comes together cohesively.

> How does Archivo's institutional position compare to other models of patronage in Mexico?

Patronage is tied to the government. The government has traditionally created and constructed culture, so it has always been understood as a public good. I think Fernando and Soumaya were smart to position Archivo first as a design space rather than an architecture space. Fernando was reluctant to address architecture because he has a specific

○
Installation view of the exhibition *One Hundred Years in One Hundred Fragments (MXCD02)*, October 13, 2017 to January 13, 2018, Archivo, Mexico City. Photograph by Rodrigo Chapa.
Image courtesy of Archivo.

vision of architecture. My labor has been to find different ways to incorporate architecture. I'm not interested, for instance, in having a model show on contemporary Mexican architects. Curation resolves itself in the difficult negotiation of who is behind the show, how you focus the project, and how you turn it into something different. Negotiation happens in any institution or in any space. A curator always has to manage different interests to push the mission of the project.

> The *Centro SCOP* exhibition seemed quite complex to organize, especially in its timely response to an unexpected national catastrophe. Can you talk about how the show came together?

The *Centro SCOP* show was interesting because we put it together quickly a few weeks after the 2017 Mexico City earthquake. When architects came together to respond to the disaster, their focus was solely on housing. With thousands of people whose houses had collapsed, housing became the most evident urgent issue. But more than eight hundred historic buildings were also damaged by the earthquake. Most of them were colonial churches in the south of Mexico, close to the epicenter. For Archivo, promoting the preservation of modern architecture has been a hugely important issue—for me personally but also in the spirit of the curatorial project. The earthquake was an opportunity to confront issues we hadn't delved into and to do so with a sense of urgency, because we had only three months to put the show together. The show originated from a conversation between the artist Pedro Reyes and Fernando Romero. When the news media predicted the demolition of Centro SCOP—the former Communications Ministry building, which was completely covered in stone mosaic murals by Juan O'Gorman, José Chávez Morado, and other important twentieth-century artists and architects and had already been reconstructed after being severely damaged in another major earthquake in 1985—Pedro said, "You should take the murals to the airport, it's the only building that's big enough to hold them, and it would be amazing!" They were excited about this idea. I thought the proposition was intriguing but that we couldn't make a show out of just that idea. We decided to bring in other artists and tried to pick at the different tensions— how to preserve the building, why it was built, what its function was, why it was completely rebuilt following the 1985 earthquake. I believe these extreme environmental disasters, and the resulting questions for architecture, are going to become increasingly common. With more volatile climatic conditions and social and economic destabilization, more and more of the solutions for preserving heritage will have to deal with resolving this crisis. The show was an interesting moment to think differently about preservation, but one in which we could only ask questions for which we didn't have answers.

> As a nimble organization of three people, you each must have to wear many hats to get all the work done. These skills aren't always taught in design education. Do you believe there's also a void in teaching about alternative forms of practice, including curatorial work? What does Archivo do to challenge this issue?

Our most direct connection to education is through our intern program. We have a tiny army of ten new interns every six months. At the beginning it was difficult, but now we have a good understanding of how to introduce students to this world. They're part of the research, the display production, the communication. Their experience at Archivo helps to fill in gaps that aren't necessarily addressed in school. For us, this has been an easy way of creating closer connections with schools and offering alternatives to thinking about design education in Mexico.

ON AUTHORSHIP

In your lecture preceding this conversation, you mentioned that architects in Mexico don't like showing works in progress, yet Archivo organized and exhibited the *Design in Process* show. Can you elaborate on why you believe Mexican architects resist showing their process?

In Mexico, many people think that everyone else is stealing their work. The *Design in Process* show was interesting because we had projects that were so similar in their materiality. For that show, I worked with the architect-trained contemporary artist Isauro Huizar. His idea was that the show wouldn't be about the projects themselves but about what the projects share. This is what Hegel would call "the spirit of the times"—as in, how do you get a sense of what's happening generally? Why are people reacting to certain conditions in a similar way? The format of that exhibition was a straightforward way of getting at those questions. It was already difficult to read because the architects' projects were fragmented into samples and models, and we made it even more difficult by separating the pieces. For instance, we placed similar materials from different projects on one table and pieces with the same structural logic on another table. The format enabled us to ask firms to send us whatever was on their desk, mix it all up, and then provide them with a different reading of their work.

In general, we like to challenge assumptions about design. Authorship and originality are huge assumptions. Some participants couldn't even identify where the pieces of their projects were. Others were disappointed because their authorship wasn't explicitly communicated.

Questions surrounding authorship and originality aren't typically articulated in Mexico in the ways that seem to be more common in Europe or the United States. European and U.S. institutions have these exercises and discussions in school, while Mexican design institutions focus on production. Within Mexican design education, there's little criticism, practically no general history, and literally no history of Mexican design. Students don't have a clue about who came before them. That's what we try to address at Archivo and with this show.

In your lecture you discussed works where the author is unknown and how you've had to develop strategies for dealing with these difficult questions of authorship. What are those strategies?

A large proportion of our collection is anonymous design. One example of how we've approached this is the *silla Corona*, or Corona chair—basically a folding metal chair with "Corona," the name of the beer, inscribed on it. They're ubiquitous in Mexico because the beer company that produces Corona gives them away as publicity, so you see bars and cantinas full of them. One of the first research projects initiated by Archivo's previous director, Regina Pozo, was a genealogy of the Corona chair. O   She connected it to constructivism, to ideas of industrial standardization, and to the need for low-cost furniture for massive public events.

This way of reading and analyzing the collective history of an object and its authorship can be difficult when some of the objects, especially industrial objects, don't have an archival history. For example, Mexico used to have an amazing Knoll factory—the building was designed by Félix Candela—but the company discarded its archive about ten or fifteen years ago. The factory lost the license to produce Knoll chairs in the 1980s, but they still had the original molds, so they started bootlegging them. The end product was no longer officially Knoll, even though they were using the original molds. The history of this sort of phenomenon, for example, had been largely lost.

MARIO BALLESTEROS

○
Installation view of the exhibition *One Hundred Years in One Hundred Fragments (MXCD02)*, October 13, 2017 to January 13, 2018, Archivo, Mexico City. Photograph by Rodrigo Chapa.
Image courtesy of Archivo.

ON AUTHORSHIP

There's this sense of urgency now, because culture is being discarded and lost at a pace that is probably unique to our time. It took longer for things to be considered archaic, useless, or trash fifty years ago. However, we, as an institution and society, shouldn't become hoarders. You can't say, "Oh, I have to have every single Walkman that ever existed, because they're going extinct." But there is that strange sort of place for what is important to keep and to recover.

Giving young designers a space or voice via an exhibition or an acquisition can change the trajectory of their careers. Can you discuss Archivo's role as a platform for showing the work of young designers or informal creators? What's your relationship with young designers in Mexico City and beyond? How do you choose who gets a show and who doesn't?

Fernando has always thought of Archivo as a space for young architects and designers, which I completely believe in as well. The philosophy has been to exhibit and publish either first works or designers who haven't been published before. For me, that has been part of the mission of these independent spaces. If you can't open spaces to people who normally wouldn't have that opportunity, what's the point of a different space?

Also, young architects in Mexico can be fresh out of school and already have a practice because of the structure of the educational model. You can start building when you're still in school; you don't need to be licensed to build a house in Mexico. That's part of this unique, strange context to which we need to find a way to respond. For me, it's important to be as open as we can in how we select works. We always try to find a different person, a different perspective. I don't think anyone's had two exhibition displays at Archivo. Every exhibition is an opportunity to open a space for a different perspective, and that's been a guideline for us. ○

Can you describe some examples of the different perspectives you invite to Archivo; for example, in the *Design in Process* show (2016), which focused on the developmental stages of work by young Mexican designers?

The *Design in Process* show was interesting because it initiated future collaborations. We researched and invited about one hundred designers and offices throughout the country to send us their current work. In the end, we selected about forty designers for the show. The three young architecture practices that we commissioned for the Mexico Design City (MXDC) series—Escobedo Soliz and Eugenio Rebolleda, Tezontle Studio, and PALMA—came out of that earlier open call. The commission process varies—some are direct, and sometimes we think of completed work that resonates. In the case of the MXDC series, we had commissioned Tezontle Studio for a previous show with objects including a cabinet of curiosities. They have an aesthetic that's

MARIO BALLESTEROS

○
Exterior view of the Archivo space during the exhibition *MXCD02*,
October 13, 2017 to January 13, 2018, Archivo, Mexico City. Photograph
by Rodrigo Chapa.
Image courtesy of Archivo.

reminiscent of Mexican museums from the 1950s, and so we thought they would be perfect for the MXDC show. But we consciously try to bring in new people all the time.

> As part of your role as director, you relaunched Archivo's website, which has become a robust digital platform for communicating your mission. Can you talk about how the website furthers Archivo's work?

I think the website is important. The house, the actual physical space that Archivo occupies, was the first important step for us. When I joined, half of the space—including the storage rooms for the collection—wasn't open to the public. The first thing I did was open and activate every nook and cranny of the house. Now the storage areas are open to the public, and people walk around our office all the time, asking us, "What's this? Can I buy something?" We created the little reading room, the library—these very physical distributions of functions and of what we offer.

So now the website is structured like the space. Both the physical and digital spaces are organized by these words: *space*, *collecting*, *exhibiting*, *rethinking*. I think our digital presence is going to be just as important as the physical space, because we need additional outlets for the research and work we produce.

> Can you talk about this idea of rethinking and how it manifests at Archivo? You seem to demonstrate this idea with how you exhibit work—for example, the open archive where people can interact with and touch objects—but also through historical investigations and the ways in which you make this research accessible to the public. Do you see these instances of rethinking as manifesting primarily for your audience, or during your research and curation, or as a mix of the two?

Archivo's mission statement is clear, except for the part on rethinking and its purpose, which is intentionally fuzzy. For us, *rethinking* is a concentration of all the strange things we do and the particularities of our institution. It captures a way of thinking beyond exhibitions. Yes, exhibitions have been what our audience traditionally expects from Archivo, but we acknowledge that there's much more to an exhibition than just the show. There's what comes before and what is left after the show. For us, that's just as important and interesting as the show itself. The research is what comes before. The show is not just the public program but also the lectures, workshops, and discussions that take place over the duration of an exhibition. Then there's the registration of everything, which is what's left after. For example, for all of our architecture and art books in the Archivo series, we've commissioned new texts after the exhibition. An exhibition opens up new questions that we weren't able to address initially, so we commission a text afterward from someone who's working on the issue in question.

Rethinking is the underlying spirit of everything we do. It includes the things that don't fit necessarily into one of the more conventional institutional categories—exhibiting or collecting. I'm hoping that this spirit is going to become our archive, that it's going to become Archivo. ○   If you explore the Rethinking section on our website, you see that it can include opinion pieces, reviews, or just photos of a get-together. Part of rethinking is just *reuniones*—meetings. It can be as simple as having a discussion over some drinks. For example, we've had a habit of "poaching" cool people who are visiting Mexico. We invite them to have a mezcal, and we get together a group of ten or fifteen designers

MARIO BALLESTEROS

○
Installation views of the exhibition *Archivo Italia*, October 22, 2015 to
January 15, 2016, Archivo, Mexico City. Photographs by PJ Rountree.
Images courtesy of Archivo.

who we think could have an interesting conversation with them. We've hosted Jonathan Olivares, Beatrice Leanza, and Adam Greenfield—people we couldn't fly in ourselves. They love the format because it's an intimate exchange. Jonathan, for example, presented his new book by walking the group through it instead of giving a talk. That, for me, is rethinking. It's about how we can go beyond what is expected of an exhibition or a research space. It addresses how you can think of design differently, which is what underlies everything else for us.

> Your description of the website leads to a question about media and afterlives. Can you talk about how you approach documenting a show as a small organization, whether through the website or through physical media?

I think that next step has been where we've struggled the most, because we don't have the resources, time, or people to make everything work. We've struggled with publishing the books, because we need to keep pushing the exhibition program. Redesigning the website became a priority because we had been operating in a new direction for three years and no one knew about it with our older website. It's a slow process. While our exhibitions are super quick, the rest has been slow, difficult, and exhausting. For me, the life after the exhibition is the next challenge. I can't *not* get those books out; we couldn't *not* have a website. I think that's really where you start to see the limits of the Archivo project.

> In contrast to this slowness, you've also emphasized the speed of the exhibition program at Archivo, where the sheer quantity and variety of exhibitions you've produced generates an enormous amount of energy. How does the speed of the exhibitions relate to your approach to curation? With this shift into the different temporality of the website, does the digital space become an alternative curatorial platform?

When I came to Archivo, there wasn't a program, and I didn't understand how exhibitions were put together before me. Eventually I understood that they were put together a few weeks beforehand and that it was an intensive, chaotic process. The first thing I tried to do was introduce order to the process. From that point, we were going to program the exhibitions, generate the context, and do the research. It was a way to test our own muscle, and we've exhausted that muscle after two years. The *One Hundred Years in One Hundred Fragments* exhibition was insane to do with a tiny team doing research, production, and everything else. I'm comfortable with where we are in terms of defining the curatorial spirit of what we do at Archivo. I feel like we've pretty much solved it. Now the huge challenge is making it sustainable.

Mario Ballesteros is currently an independent design and architecture curator and editor. This conversation took place in September 2018, before Archivo Diseño y Arquitectura closed as a public exhibition space in summer 2019.

SHIRLEY SURYA

CURATING AS COLLECTION-BUILDING

How does your curatorial approach reflect M+'s unique situation in Hong Kong?

For M+, or any museum in the world, the main audience is naturally based on where the institution is located. As a museum based in Hong Kong, M+ inevitably relates to the Hong Kong audience and the region of greater China. But because Hong Kong is also known for being transnational and porous—historically a cultural and economic gateway to China, Asia, and the world—M+'s collecting approach is inevitably regional and global as much as it is local. As a colonial, postcolonial, or neocolonial city, Hong Kong has never held an allegiance to a single entity.

M+ has actively sought to establish itself amid a field of local, regional, and international institutions focused on architecture and design. Whom do you see as your peer institutions, and how does M+ differentiate itself from these institutions?

Locally, M+ is the only museum that collects design and architecture in addition to visual art and the moving image, all of which are part of its remit as a visual culture museum. This is the main distinctive feature of M+ compared to museums regionally and globally. Our global, transnational, and multidisciplinary remit may be similar to collecting institutions like the Museum of Modern Art in New York, the Victoria and Albert Museum in London, and the National Museum of Modern and Contemporary Art in Seoul. Our international ambition and interest in both art and design are also similar to (largely) noncollecting, exhibition-making institutions like the Mori Art Museum in Tokyo and the Power Station of Art in Shanghai. However, we differ from these institutions in our regional commitment to building a collection focused on Asia. While institutions like the Asian Art Museum in San Francisco, the Fukuoka Asian Art Museum, or the National Gallery Singapore (which focuses on Southeast Asia) have a similar regional focus, the fact that M+ also acquires design and architecture is a major factor differentiating us.

> Are there formalized collaborations between M+ and other institutions?

In terms of programming, yes. The M+ International series that launched in 2019 is co-organized with partner institutions. Collaborating with like-minded institutions of similar scale, with similar disciplinary or regional interests is important in positioning M+ in relation to other peer institutions. We collaborated with the Sydney Opera House on a music and moving image festival for which our moving image co-curator, Ulanda Blair, curated a piece that was projected onto the Opera House. With the Mori Art Museum in Tokyo we collaborated on a symposium in which we asked what it means to build a collection in the twenty-first century. A third collaboration was a hybrid online/offline symposium involving Archigram and Mainland Chinese architects co-organized with the Power Station of Art. The most recent M+ International event was a series of conversations on pandemic-era programming and collection-building with the National Gallery Singapore.

Apart from a couple of programs—namely, "Rethinking Pei: A Centenary Symposium," organized with the Harvard Graduate School of Design and the University of Hong Kong Department of Architecture, and the exhibition *Noguchi for Danh Vo: Counterpoint*, organized with the Noguchi Museum—since 2012 M+ largely hasn't collaborated with other institutions on exhibitions. That's because we wanted to carve out an identity and curatorial approach by staging our own exhibitions based on the collection we've built thus far.

CURATING AS COLLECTION-BUILDING

What have been the challenges in, or responses to, M+ acquiring key archives from various countries in Asia? For instance, M+ acquired the personal archive of Wang Dahong (1917–2018) after the National Taiwan Museum had already received his drawing archive.

In collecting significant architectural archives, we've faced distrust and resistance, largely based on differing views of what an international museum should collect or a limited perception of M+ as a museum focusing on Asia but with a global purview. Some have accused us of being "neocolonialist," likening us to European or American institutions acquiring works from Asia. Others with nationalistic positions thought we shouldn't acquire any works that tell the story of nation-building in other countries in Southeast Asia, because those materials should be collected by their own national museums. Some of these critics even went as far as notifying their own ministries of culture and heritage about M+'s acquisition plans and asking them to start building national collections so these materials would remain in their own countries.

While some may feel the same way about us acquiring the archive of Wang Dahong from

Taiwan, it was ultimately the Wang family who entrusted us with their father's personal archive of photographs, sketches, ephemera, and letters. ○ Wang's drawings were already part of the National Taiwan Museum's collection, thanks to the efforts of a group of architectural historians in Taiwan.

Now that we've cataloged some of our archives, these materials have become available on the M+ Collections website, and people have started using them. One example is our holdings for Architects Team 3/Lim Chong Keat, an important architectural practice active from the late 1950s through the late 1980s in Singapore and Malaysia. People started diving into this archive and reposting the materials we digitized through a popular Instagram account, Modernist Architecture Singapore, which in turn drew more people to the archive. We hope everyone eventually realizes that M+ doesn't collect for ourselves. The works we acquire are available to everyone for reference online or physically at our Research Centre. We're not collecting for the sake of prestige but to conserve and catalog material for future research and knowledge dissemination.

As a new institution, it's notable that M+ distinguishes architecture and design as one of its three disciplines of focus,

○
Wang Dahong. *Photograph, Wang Dahong and his Voisin car (Avions Voisin C25) in Paris, 1937*, 1937. Gelatin silver print, sheet: 21 × 27.8 cm. M+, Hong Kong. Gift of Family of Wang Dahong, 2016. [CA30/5/2/1]. © Family of Wang Dahong.

○
M+ museum in Hong Kong's West Kowloon Cultural District, designed by Herzog & de Meuron.
Images courtesy of M+.

alongside visual art and the moving image.
How did architecture and design become
one of these three focal disciplines?

M+ is built on reclaimed land in West Kowloon,
Hong Kong. ○   When the West Kowloon Cultural
District, of which M+ is a part, was initially
planned in the early 2000s, the idea was to pair
developers and architects who would then set up
museums like the Guggenheim or The Met. Public
outcry questioned why museums should be developed this way rather than being built from scratch.
Consequently, a Museums Advisory Group (MAG)
came together to consider what such a new museum
might look like, based on its location in Hong Kong,
and to rethink the disciplines this museum should
contain. How could it become an institution unlike
any other museum? The MAG published its recommendations in 2006; they coined "Museum Plus"
(M+) to mean "more than a museum or building
space." MAG's main recommendation was that M+
be a museum for "visual culture," encompassing
not only visual art but also design, architecture, the
moving image, and aspects of popular culture—as
these were key aspects of Hong Kong's cultural
production. This remit was the main attraction for
the founding director of M+, Lars Nittve, the former

director of Moderna Museet in Stockholm and founding director of the Tate Modern in London.

I was the first curator hired for the M+ design and architecture team. Before that I was a journalist and writer for design and architecture magazines and was going through Yung Ho Chang's archive for his retrospective in Beijing after finishing my master's in the history of design (with a focus on architecture and Asia) at the Royal College of Art. This background influenced how I interpreted and approached M+'s institutional remit. I applied because I was excited by the potential of M+ as a museum in Asia that cares about design—which was an absolute rarity. The efforts M+ was taking to develop an interdisciplinary framework were also exciting to me. During my interview, Lars and Tobias Berger (the managing curator of M+ at the time) asked me two very thoughtful questions. The first was on how design could relate to the moving image and visual art. They knew they wanted curators who had a deep knowledge of a discipline but were also able to think laterally, who were interested to engage with other disciplines. The second question asked about my thoughts on when modern design began in China, as a way of asking how one would build a collection of twentieth- and twenty-first-century design and architecture in Asia.

It became apparent that we, as individual curators, would have to elaborate on and shape the recommendations laid out in MAG's 2006 paper. Lars, however, made the executive decision that visual art, design and architecture, and the moving image would form the three key disciplines that would structure the curatorial team. Nine months after me, Aric Chen was hired to lead the design and architecture team. Since Aric and I were both steeped in architecture, it became as important an area of focus as design.

How have you developed acquisition protocols within M+'s mission as a trans-national institution? How do you decide what to collect?

The M+ curatorial team is to a certain degree unified in our acquisition agenda. But at the same time, we each have a different focus. Collecting may seem systematic, but it's not a science. It's highly seren-dipitous—you could be actively trying to find collec-tions or pieces that you can't actually get, either due to availability or legal ownership issues. Sometimes something rare and unplanned comes up that meets our collecting goals, and we have to decide whether to acquire it. The decision is often made based on the will of a single curator, although if it's a more complex and costly acquisition it would need a collective endorsement. All proposed acquisitions also have to go through formal approval by the Acquisitions Committee—and this process is out-lined online.

The more challenging, and at the same time illuminating, part of the acquisition process can be seen in the debates we held and the criteria we eventually arrived at for building the design and ar-chitecture collections. In the beginning, Aric—who now directs Het Nieuwe Instituut in Rotterdam—

○
Ron Arad. *Rover Chair (3.5 liter one-seater)*, 1981. Leather imitation, metal, foam, plastic, and lacquered steel, overall: 74.5 × 70.5 × 93.4 cm. M+, Hong Kong. [2012.1630]. © Ron Arad.

and I argued quite a bit on how to begin building the collection. For instance, he wanted to acquire a 1981 *Rover Chair* by British industrial designer Ron Arad. ○   I questioned it as M+'s first design object, especially when our collection ought to focus on Asia. Aric argued that the *Rover Chair* was a car seat turned into a chair and that the idea of using a found object as a design strategy was reflective of comparable phenomena in Asia. For Aric, it wasn't so much about the work or the object coming from Asia or having been made by someone in Asia— though these remain key criteria—but rather how an object from elsewhere presents parallels, affinities, or similar patterns of production with those common in this part of the world. Increasingly, I was convinced such an approach would enable M+ to illuminate larger phenomena across regional, national, and cultural borders. It has thus become one of the key strategies for how we acquire works—even in the other disciplines—that aren't from Asia.

Aric and I also differed on the question of whether we should refrain from acquiring works from galleries or works that are considered collector's items, especially when they are pricey. My view was that we should instead aim for objects that other institutions in the world don't collect.

I hold these views quite strongly as a historian. I'm most passionate about searching for noncanonical objects and primary archival sources from regions with underrepresented design and architecture histories, like Southeast Asia. But I quickly realized that M+ needs to focus on both the canonical and the noncanonical, and that M+ can create an expanded discourse when we bring into dialogue the known and the lesser-known, which in effect also means engaging multiple audiences, both the scholarly and the wider public. Eventually, I was convinced of the value of such a diverse and collective approach to institution building.

> In your work on the architect William S.M. Lim, included in the exhibition *Incomplete Urbanism: Attempts of Critical Spatial Practice* (2016–2017) at the NTU Centre for Contemporary Art Singapore, you describe Lim and his contemporaries as searching for an "Asian specificity" in their work. Can you discuss what this idea of "Asian specificity" means for your curatorial practice?

I understood Lim's writings as being characterized by a search for "Asian specificity," meaning they look into a regional and contextual set of conditions.

SHIRLEY SURYA

○
Installation views of the exhibition *Incomplete Urbanism: Attempts of Critical Spatial Practice*, October 29, 2016 to January 29, 2017, NTU Centre for Contemporary Art Singapore,
Images courtesy of NTU Centre for Contemporary Art Singapore.

○   In my own practice, especially when I'm researching architectural production across Asia, I also look for similar conditions. So "Asian" is not so much an essentialist approach. The first M+ Matters symposium Aric and I organized was "Asian Design: Histories, Collecting, Curating," which was intended to critically probe what "Asian design" is. *Asian* is a term we cannot do away with, so we used the symposium to address its significance and limitations. I always encourage my colleagues not to use the term *Asian* but instead to describe works or practitioners "in Asia"; that is, to focus on "Asia" as a geographical entity as opposed to "Asian," which is a descriptor that embodies an assumed set of characteristics. The borders in the region of Asia are porous. *Asian* suggests a unified characteristic, but Asia is diverse; it's neither static nor monolithic.

By using the neutrality of geography, we can involve many more participants in our curatorial narratives, including architects like Frank Lloyd Wright and Paul Rudolph who built projects in Asia. Seeing Asia as a geographical entity, we also avoid associating the region with a form or style and can address instead a more dynamic set of conditions. *Conditions* suggests things that are consistent across a region, like climate or colonialism, but can also mean aspects that are completely tumultuous. We value practices that are sensitive to shaping those conditions. We have to consider local, translocal, national, and transnational forces, which aren't static. For instance, there are different conditions within the localities of a single nation. While researching the region's nation-building projects, we realized the production of these works and their aspirations were highly transnational and internationalist, even if they were nationalistic in origin. We want to bring up these tensions. We don't want to simplify the complex nature of these conditions and suggest there's only one way of looking at them. So we consider specificity as something that is not to be assumed and encourage others—the audience or fellow researchers—to look deeper.

> You contrast M+'s transnational model with the nationalist missions that typify many other museums in the region. Can you talk about these nationalist frameworks?

At its extreme, a nationalistic framework uncritically glorifies the history of a nation, such that a national museum won't consider an exhibition if it doesn't focus on or praise the country it's based in. Nationalism can also manifest as a narrative that claims creativity came out of the context of a nation in isolation. A transnational perspective, on the other hand, would seek to trace how canonical artists in China, for instance, were trained in and shaped by what was happening in Paris or Tokyo. We want to be aware of such influences, as well as the transformations that occur as ideas travel across borders, rather than attributing creativity to a single source of nationalistic inspiration. What underpins a transnational framework is also the acknowledgment that the creative aspiration toward a common humanity trumps the dominance of any single territory.

> How does this thinking affect M+ in terms of its current situation in Hong Kong, as a Special Administrative Region of the People's Republic of China, especially with regard to concerns over the recently passed National Security Law?

The National Security Law (NSL) is ambiguous, and nobody knows how it will be exercised, especially in relation to artistic production. When it was first introduced, we held an event with the directors of four museums in China: the Power Station of Art, the UCCA Center for Contemporary Art in Beijing, the Times Museum in Guangzhou, and the Rockbund Art Museum in Shanghai, all of which are among the boldest curatorial institutions in China. We asked them to tell us what they expect from M+ as we open our building to the public this year. The founding artistic director of the UCCA, Fei Dawei, said, "My impression of Hong Kong is that it's a little bit full of stricture. I'm not sure where M+ will be able to transcend this, but I hope you all do." That's from someone who is close to the strongholds of power in Beijing! It's easy for us to assume limitations based on self-censorship or an exaggeration of the effects these regulations have over us. Calls to not organize exhibitions or promote works that directly incite hatred of or opposition to the government are heard in many other countries besides China.

As curators, we believe the NSL shouldn't restrict us, but at the same time the current political climate means we have to be extremely sensitive to a host of public queries and concerns, even if they don't necessarily affect how M+ moves forward. M+ is a publicly funded institution, so it's only right for us not to blatantly present content that leads to unnecessary controversy; we must make calculated decisions about why we put what we put in the gallery. For the opening of the museum, we conducted a risk assessment for every work on display. Risk assessment here doesn't just include political sensitivities but also questions of animal rights, gender, and other sociocultural issues that institutions across the globe also face. We always have to manage threats to our freedom of expression in many forms, not just the political ones.

Our stance now is to keep going until the door is shut. There's no point in wavering on our decisions. We just have to go with them and believe in them, because the narratives we are presenting in the opening displays have been planned since 2016. We're installing them in a different moment, though, so we have to be prepared for diverse and extreme responses. As much as we have people who support, affirm, and assure us, these issues still affect us. We're not saying we know what's going to happen in the future, as the ground is still shifting, but we can't operate according to what we don't know.

SHIRLEY SURYA

> When the museum began thinking about
> its collection strategies, was there an initial
> impulse to focus on archives?

Archives document the process of architectural
production, not just mere representation. My
curatorial colleagues, however, have varying views
on the value of archives, especially in the realm of
visual art, where the work itself speaks more to
the idea than to the work's archival documentation.
But artistic practice is getting increasingly diverse.
In the beginning of building the architecture
collection, we faced some resistance to acquiring
archives, because they're difficult to display. When
you're part of a museum of visual culture on such
a massive scale, one where the architecture and
design collections exist in parallel with visual art
and the moving image, the question of how the
audience will relate to what's on display is real.
Works on paper are indeed more challenging to
engage with. But we decided we needed to take
the risk for the sake of diversifying the narrative
through these primary sources. For example, while
we had doubts about acquiring the archive of
Tao Ho— a Harvard graduate and an influential
architect in Hong Kong—which consists mainly of
slides, photographs, and documentation, we went

ahead with displaying these materials for our first exhibition of the architecture collection. We were heartened by the attention visitors paid to both the archival documentation and tangible models and the 1:1 installation.

As we came to understand the need for M+ to contribute to historicizing cultural production across Asia, we increasingly saw the value of the archive—a source of primary documents—as a vehicle for research and display within this larger project. You can acquire a model or a one-to-one mock-up, or you can try to impress the audience with your space or exhibition design, but you can't necessarily expand or construct histories through these means. When you acquire an archive, you have the potential to collect material that nobody has written about before, and that's where M+ can contribute to ongoing efforts to expand and interrogate the canon. Our decision to acquire the Archigram archive was a culmination of this realization about the importance of archives.

> What is your attitude toward the status of these archival materials as "original" artifacts, versus other forms of display that can communicate their information to audiences?

SHIRLEY SURYA

The decision of what to acquire is often linked to the issue of display. Acquiring original architectural models or fragments would pose no issue in how we display them. As for archival materials, while we would like to display the materials as they are— be it slides, photographs, or drawings—sometimes the materials aren't in a suitable condition for display. Then we choose to reproduce them for ease of view or for conservation purposes. Our decision to reproduce models is where we differ with most collecting institutions, which value the authenticity or historicity of the object. Due to poor archival practices and scarcity of space for storing models, few original architectural models exist for us to acquire. Yet the model is a key way for the public to understand the nature of the work. So we decided to commission reproductions for the collection based on a set of criteria we established. For example, the model has to be reproduced by the original architect(s) based on available drawings or photographs of the original model or on a study of the building as it was realized.

> Can you discuss the process and decisions around M+'s acquisition of the Archigram archive, especially in terms of your interests as a Hong Kong-based institution with a global perspective?

The acquisition of the Archigram archive by M+ was a result of Aric Chen's persuasion. Acquiring their archive was an institutional feat, not just because of the cost but because several institutions in Europe and the United States were also competing for it. ○   Justifying why we should acquire the archive and negotiating the cost with Archigram to a level that was acceptable to us took almost four years. For every prospective acquisition, we have to raise the question of relevance and relationship, not just with creative production in Asia but with the rest of the M+ collection. In this case, Aric had to rally all of our stakeholders, including the Acquisitions Committee, explaining to them how the Archigram archive was important to Hong Kong, Asia, and M+ as a regionally focused institution with a global perspective.

     The "Archigram Cities" symposium we organized in 2020 was the beginning of our attempt to grapple with the question of Archigram's relationship with, and impact on, Asia across time, disciplines, and geographies. ○   The program reflected our desire to incite a productive dialogue on the parallels and dissonances with Archigram's ideas. We invited scholars and practitioners from the region who weren't directly related to, or necessarily interested in, Archigram's work. Liam Young, for example, has

○
Unpacking a drawing from Archigram's Rent-a-Wall in the M+ storage.
Photograph © M+, Hong Kong (top).
"Archigram Cities" symposium, November 2020 (bottom).
Image courtesy of Shirley Surya.

a background in cinematic game design. We were curious how he would engage with the work of Archigram and how his perspective might differ from that of a scholar like Lai Chee Kien, who has studied Archigram's design for the *Instant Malaysia* exhibition in London (1973) through a postcolonial lens. We also invited some of the more influential architects from Mainland China, including Meng Yan of Urbanus and Ma Yansong, who believe in Archigram's spirit—either in applying the Instant City approach in the ad hoc context of China or in engaging architecture with fantastical yet urgent solutions to today's urban challenges. We see these dialogues as a way of prompting deeper consideration of how we could use the acquisition of Archigram's archive to further historicize or dismantle current understandings and applications of Archigram's diverse approaches.

Another reason for the relevance of the Archigram archive to M+ is that we consider Archigram's work to be part of visual cultural production, not just architecture. As a museum collecting visual art, design and architecture, and the moving image, we value Archigram's practice not only on the level of its structural, spatial, and urban propositions but for how it engaged with meaning- and image-making through publications, exhibitions, film, and happenings that came out of a highly vibrant interdisciplinary artistic scene in the United Kingdom and Europe. Archigram has had a definite relationship with, and influence on, representational practices not just within architecture but also in other disciplines.

> You mentioned that sometimes your commitment as an institution in Hong Kong can include reinterpreting projects by non-Asian designers who have relationships with the region. How do you think about other artifacts by canonical European or North American authors in the M+ collections; for example, your archive of Frank Lloyd Wright's drawings for the Imperial Hotel in Tokyo? Is it a goal of M+ to decolonize these objects?

The idea of engaging a broad audience is always key for us. We can't deny that Frank Lloyd Wright rings a bell for the non-architects in our audience. In this respect, we understand that we can't deny the canon. Nor can we deny that the history of architecture here is highly intertwined with and influenced by ideas from particular institutions or practitioners in the United States and Europe. We don't use the

THE IMPORTANCE OF THE ARCHIVE

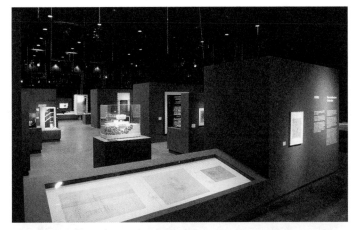

○

Building M+: The Museum and Architecture Collection, January 10 to February 9, 2014, ArtisTree, Hong Kong (top).
In Search of Southeast Asia through the M+ Collections, June 22 to September 30, 2018 at M+ (bottom).
Photographs © M+, Hong Kong.

word *decolonizing* or the term *revisionist*, as these can be misunderstood as purely oppositional and risk creating another form of centering and marginalization. We'd rather describe our approach as expanding or pluralizing the canon. We're porous to both the canonical and the noncanonical—we can't engage one without the other.

We acquired Wright's drawings of the Imperial Hotel in Tokyo and included them in the exhibition *Building M+: The Museum and Architecture Collection* (2014) largely due to their significance as an early form of transnational production. ○ The drawings represented the narrative of Wright having to revise his design based on his collaboration with local artisans and the availability of building materials. This story of exchanges, cross-cultural influences, and transformation speaks to M+ as an institution based in Hong Kong, a site that has experienced similar patterns of cultural production. This perspective has also informed our acquisition of works by Paul Rudolph that document his practice in Hong Kong, Singapore, and Indonesia.

Do your collections of twentieth-century architecture focus on the modern movement or on other periods as well? How do you approach the fact that certain periodizing styles or categories, like postmodernism, are often framed through a cultural/geo-graphic lens that is highly specific to Europe and the United States?

While the curators at M+ hold diverse views of what characterizes "modernism," some of us, in particular those on the design and architecture team, believe in tracing the varying effects of modernity and modernization on cultural produc-tion, as opposed to focusing our interest on a particular stylistic manifestation of the modern. Due to my previous research on communist architectural production in China from 1949 to 1979, I've challenged the need for the design and archi-tecture team to consider socialist modernism as an important area to represent in the collection. This all-embracing stance applies to our interest in postmodernism in Asia. While postmodernism has been "condemned" as a stylistic movement by certain collecting institutions, we see it as an important phase that pluralized design production and shaped design's diverse manifestations today. While the progenitors and discursive markers of postmodernism originated in Europe and the States, we're interested in the agents from Asia who were part of that discourse and production. For example, designers like Kuromata Shiro and Masanori Umeda, who were part of Memphis. We're also interested in practitioners and works that reinterpreted postmodernist strategies in ways that are specific to their cultural contexts; for example, how architects in South and Southeast Asia reconsidered and applied historical precedents in ways that are more than exercises in semiotics but rather evince pragmatic climatic design approaches.

> M+ has acquired both the work of transnational figures working in Asia and the archives of architects from Asia who worked outside the region. One example is Wang Chiu-Hwa (1925–2021), a Taiwanese architect who designed numerous buildings while working for Percival Goodman in New York prior to her return to Taiwan. Can you discuss the acquisition of her archive?

We didn't acquire Wang Chiu-Hwa's archive because she practiced in the United States but because she established an exemplary practice of her own—as a female architect—both in the United States and in Taiwan. ○   The process did raise the question of what it would mean to incorporate an archive with a large quantity of materials from North America.

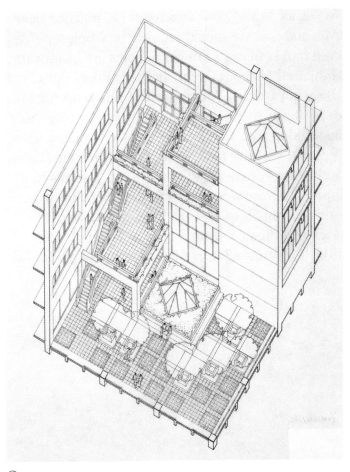

○
Wang Chiu-Hwa, J. J. Pan and Partners. Axonometric drawing, *Main Library, National Changhua University of Education (1986–1989), Chang-hua (Changhua), Taiwan* [ca. 1986 to ca. 1989]. Blackline print and marker ink on transparent paper, sheet: 29.9 × 41.9 cm. M+, Hong Kong. Gift of Wang Chiu-Hwa, 2017. [CA39/4/6/2/5]. © Wang Chiu-Hwa.

We decided this was indicative of her practice, however, and that we should acquire the whole archive, even if only five or so of her projects are in Taiwan, compared to about twenty in the United States. The acquisition of Wang's archive was an example of M+ acquiring a practitioner's entire archive—as opposed to archival materials related to one or a few projects. We have to be selective in acquiring such archives, as processing them usually entails a huge amount of resources. Apart from Wang Chiu-Hwa, other examples of such archives are those of Architects Team 3 from Singapore, Wang Dahong from Taiwan, and Sumet Jumsai from Thailand.

NEW MEDIA FOR NEW AUDIENCES

Can you talk about the primary goals of M+ prior to the construction of the building (which opens in November 2021) and how you conceived the Mobile M+ series that preceded the museum building itself?

There were three reasons for the Mobile M+ setup. First, without a building, the staff had to figure out flexible exhibitions at various sites for a few years until the new building by Herzog & de Meuron was ready. Second, we were still in the process of building our collection. So from 2011 to 2013, we displayed only commissioned works for the first two Mobile M+ exhibitions. Third, the idea of being "mobile" expressed our founding director Lars Nittve's belief that a museum is more than a building; it's about the connection and relationships between the audience and the work or content the museum presents. The first Mobile M+ exhibition was focused on Yau Ma Tei, a highly eclectic historic neighborhood in Kowloon. The project mirrored a biennial model, where we commissioned artists and architects to produce site-specific works in the neighborhood.

In contrast to the importance of archival collections for M+ as an institution, what is

your take on exhibiting architecture online
and on the presence of M+ in the digital
realm?

Patricio del Real invited me to address this question
for a series of reflective essays in the *Journal of the
Society of Architectural Historians* responding to
the COVID-19 pandemic. Of the multiple curators
who responded, we were all consistent in saying
there's no substitute for the physical exhibition. The
exhibition space has its own power, effects, and
roles to play. In that sense, there will be no change
to the physicality of exhibition spaces.

M+ doesn't believe in virtual museums as
such, but we now intend to challenge ourselves by
treating the online exhibition as its own genre. For
instance, interactive articles in the *New York Times*
are actually quite effective as online exhibitions—
they're well designed, accessible on your cellphone,
have high engagement with the audience, and have
relevant and rich content. How is this format less of
an exhibition than a physical exhibition? There are
differences, of course, but online exhibitions should
be designed and curated as their own medium.
We don't believe they should try to replicate the
experience of the physical exhibition. For now, we're
trying to challenge ourselves to make something

specific to the medium, as a way to extend our content from the exhibition spaces into other media that can reach people who aren't in Hong Kong.

> Can you describe the exhibition *Mobile M+: NEONSIGNS.HK* (2014), for which you created a digital presence to get people invested in supporting the museum?

The exhibition on neon signs gave us a distinct view of what M+ could offer, long before we had a building for the museum. We understood how neon signs have been a pervasive medium across the disciplines of visual art, the moving image, and design and architecture. We realized we could explore the neon sign as a form of endangered craft, for the ways it contributed to the distinct atmosphere of Wong Kar-wai's films through Christopher Doyle's cinematography, or for how contemporary artists have employed neon in their work. We also realized that the neon sign is a highly transnational artifact that manifests in distinct urban environments in Shanghai, Tokyo, or Las Vegas. Presenting the exhibition online was an experiment in audience engagement, but it was also highly appropriate as it enabled us to present content in diverse formats—for example, essays, slideshows, videos, and an interactive timeline—that could be easily disseminated.

The most successful aspect of this exhibition was our use of Instagram's geolocating feature as a medium to map hashtags. In the past few years many neon signs have disappeared, so we turned to crowdsourcing and asked our audience to help us document signs past and present. Since 2014, *NEONSIGNS.HK* has become a virtual archive of neon signs in Hong Kong. We did the work of framing the themes and types of neon signs, but our audience constructed the virtual experience and gathered the knowledge and raw material for the archive. Now you can click on the signs and learn where they are (or were), what they look like, or even filter them by category, such as signs for restaurants or massage parlors.

This exhibition helped us understand what is impactful or effective for an exhibition. Our digital team is telling us more and more that the answer to the question of impact is to program more than a physical exhibition. Our aim is to be as multiformat as possible, though we're still attached to the physical exhibition space. Exhibitions remain the most resource heavy format, as they involve the logistics and conservation of objects. At the same time, we always have to realize that the budget shouldn't be spent only on the physical exhibition but also on all these other ways we can engage diverse audiences with our content.

> As your platforms increasingly include both virtual and physical spaces, how do you view publications as a means of continuing the life of an exhibition?

Publication deadlines are always much earlier than exhibition-making deadlines. We sort the book out before finishing the exhibition, which then informs the exhibition to some degree. In some cases, what's in the publication may differ from what's in the exhibition. I don't believe in a direct replication, because they really are two different platforms. Whether we're designing for the web or a book, as much as we might want to create parallels to the physical exhibition, the book has its own life, content, and goals—many of which the physical exhibition can't achieve, and vice versa. The book has to do with the production of knowledge, because you can't just mount your research on the wall. The value of an exhibition publication is thus more than the images. For us, exhibition publications play the more specific role of a cultural artifact that documents new research and knowledge.

As M+ grows, how do you maintain the agility
of earlier exhibition formats when you were
navigating a less institutional version of
the museum? Is there a space between the
nimble and the fully institutional where M+
can operate?

I think we want to keep the agile spirit, but we
know it will be more difficult as we grow. For instance, we recently invited the artist Sheela Gowda
for a symposium and conversations on South and
Southeast Asia. She remarked on M+'s adventurous-
ness over the last few years and wondered whether
we'll still allow for the kind of artwork that's
difficult to install, that doesn't meet typical conservation requirements, as we become a more formal
museum. We want to embrace that uncertainty and
push those ideas as a curatorial team, but it may
be harder because we have to negotiate with other
teams that have equal decision-making roles. The
reason it takes three to six years to make anything
is that we're navigating objects and spaces, and we
can't underestimate the very real logistical element.

So it may be that this nimbleness is impossible now. We can perhaps keep our agility at the level
of our thinking about content and formats, but the
planning of a series of exhibitions that involves four

hundred staff and outside stakeholders becomes different. That's just the nature of museums generally, whether it's the way they're maintained or the hefty amount of funds and labor needed to care for a collection. All of this requires us to be much more organized and strategic.

The idea of informality or ephemerality isn't easy within a white box gallery where every object is insured and everything has a value attached to it. Our nimbleness may be rooted more in the diversity of activities the museum undertakes; for instance, through contributions to other venues, like the Venice Biennale. One such response is our *Mobile M+: Rover*, a container truck that's redesigned every year by an artist or an architect. It's a flexible space that can work as a gallery, classroom, or event space, and it goes to all the neighborhood schools. We're not planning to end this program once we have a building. On the contrary, it allows us to be more inclusive, to go out into the neighborhoods, and to expand our reach to people who would otherwise never visit M+. It's been a great way to engage multiple audiences on multiple levels.

Shirley Surya is Curator, Design and Architecture, at M+ in Hong Kong. This conversation took place via Zoom in April 2021.

MARTINO STIERLI

THE EXHIBITION AS RESEARCH

MARTINO STIERLI

As a curator of architecture and design, how do you establish a dialogue between the two disciplines in your exhibitions?

Architecture and design weren't always part of the same department at the Museum of Modern Art, but they have been joined since 1949. Historically, this union makes a lot of sense, because many of the key architects of the twentieth century embraced the avant-garde ethos of radically transforming society, and introducing modern design into the everyday reality of the people was one way of achieving this. For example, Marcel Breuer's *House in the Museum Garden* (1949) was intended as an advertisement to make modern architecture and design accessible to everyone, even though in some ways it was also a blueprint for the suburbanization of the United States in the postwar period (and the politics of racial segregation that it implied). ○ More recently, the disciplines have separated and specialized more, with design becoming increasingly separated from architectural discourse. That said, I think the combination still makes sense in exhibitions, where design objects are ideally suited to relate to the everyday experience of our visitors.

We often try to use design objects in our architecture exhibitions to make abstract

○
The House in the Museum Garden, The Museum of Modern Art, New York,
April 12 to October 30, 1949. © Ezra Stoller/Esto.

MARTINO STIERLI

architectural representations more directly grasp-
able for a broader audience. In *Toward a Concrete
Utopia: Architecture in Yugoslavia, 1948–1980* (2018),
for example, we had an entire section on design
objects. They gave the audience an indication of
how an abstract notion of modernity was unfolding
in everyday life. Conversely, design shows often
include architectural representations. It's not necessarily self-evident that the two realms are connected,
so it's useful to point out these relationships.

> How are architecture and design conceived
> of more broadly within the Museum of
> Modern Art as an institution?

In the beginning, there were no dedicated architecture and design galleries at MoMA, and an acquisitions committee specific to architecture and design
was only introduced in the mid-1960s. In the wake
of Clement Greenberg's thesis that the meaning of
art lay in its self-referentiality and that therefore its
ultimate objective was to achieve absolute autonomy,
the various artistic mediums became extremely
separated at MoMA. This split was also reflected in
the museum's departmental structure, where each
department became almost an independent entity
within the larger institution. The generation of chief

curators who are in charge now doesn't believe that this complete separation of disciplines makes sense anymore. At the same time, as an architectural historian, I'm very aware that architecture is its own discipline and has its own very specific narratives and methodologies.

For this reason, we used the recent expansion of the museum, which opened to the public in 2019, to fundamentally rethink how to present our collection. We developed a "both/and" approach in terms of medium-specificity. We continue to have designated galleries that are driven by architecture or design—or photography for that matter—but we also have galleries that are much more inclusive. For example, it would be absurd to curate a gallery on the Bauhaus that doesn't include painting and design in the same space, as the synthesis of these fields was a principal objective of the radical pedagogical project of the Bauhaus. The level of integration is an ongoing conversation, and not always an easy one, because architecture and design frequently respond to a different set of questions than the visual arts do. That we have a broad representation of all kinds of artistic mediums, including architecture and design, but also photography and film, is one of the great assets of the museum—and also distinguishes it from many similar institutions dedicated to modern art.

MARTINO STIERLI

○
Installation view of the exhibition *From the Collection: 1960–1969*, March
26, 2016 to March 12, 2017, The Museum of Modern Art, New York.
Photograph by Martin Seck.
Image courtesy of The Museum of Modern Art.

How did the different departments collaborate when you first began to bring media together in your exhibitions?

In 2017 my colleague Ann Temkin from the Department of Painting and Sculpture and I co-curated *From the Collection: 1960–1969*, together with a group of curators from all the curatorial departments. In this experiment, we eliminated any separation between artistic mediums or preset art-historical terms. We used the entire fourth floor and created a chronological walk-through: gallery one was for works created in the year 1960, gallery two was for 1961, gallery three was for 1962, and so on. It just so happened that we had ten galleries, so we could show the entire decade. It was interesting to see, for instance, a Jaguar E-Type car next to Robert Rauschenberg's *First Landing Jump* (1961), because suddenly you were able to relate them to each other. ○   It wasn't necessarily an ideal contextualization of the car in design history, but it was a striking representation of the zeitgeist and visual environment in which that car was designed. Sometimes we cheated a bit in the placement of material because, as we know, buildings aren't designed and executed in one year, which gave us a bit of flexibility. In some instances this fully integrated form of display worked very well, and in others we saw the limitations of what this kind of narrative could do. It remained an experiment, and we didn't pursue this kind of installation for the new presentation of the collection. However, it was a useful exercise, most importantly because it introduced an entirely new model of cross-departmental collaboration to the curatorial staff.

> For Alfred H. Barr Jr., the first MoMA director, the museum was a public laboratory, while for Arthur Drexler, the long-standing director of the Department of Architecture and Design, the museum was a venue to display "good design." What is your sense of MoMA's current take on exhibiting and collecting relative to these two positions?

I'm not entirely sure if the positions of Alfred Barr and Arthur Drexler were really so diametrically opposed. I can say that Barr's notion of the museum as a laboratory came up quite frequently in our discussions as we were envisioning the new museum, which started right around the time I came to MoMA in 2015. Conversely, the idea of "good design" was very much a part of the mission of the museum in the postwar period, where the idea was to spread the gospel of modernism and make it available and affordable to everyone. That said, Drexler certainly pursued other interests as well during his long tenure; think, for example, of his shows on visionary architecture or his seminal exhibition on the architecture of the Beaux-Arts. Drexler's increasing disenchantment with the appropriation of modernism by corporate America was manifested in the 1979 *Transformations* show. ○

As curators in the present, we're very aware of the work of our predecessors and aim to situate our exhibitions within a larger historical and institutional trajectory. We revisited the notion of "good design" in the recent *Value of Good Design* exhibition, curated by Juliet Kinchin. It wasn't merely a celebration of MoMA's earlier program to promote affordable design but a thorough investigation of the ethos of democratizing modern design in the mid-twentieth century, and it also looked at similar programs elsewhere, including Eastern Europe during the Cold War, thereby underlining our contemporary commitment to expanding the canon on a global scale. And, of course, the notion of good design is very much alive and well in the MoMA Design Store! Unlike earlier design shows, which often only presented industrially produced and readily available objects, our interest in recent years

○
Installation view of the exhibition *Transformations in Modern Architecture*,
February 21 to April 24, 1979, The Museum of Modern Art, New York (top).
Photograph by Mali Olatunji.
View of the 1998 summer DJ series "Warm Up" at PS1 (bottom).
Photograph by John Wronn.
Images courtesy of The Museum of Modern Art.

has increasingly shifted from product to process, and so our shows now often feature prototypes, material samples, and the like, thereby highlighting the often experimental aspect of design.

At the same time, we remain fully committed to contemporary discourse and production in both architecture and design, where the experimental and the notion of the laboratory are still active. The recent Neri Oxman retrospective (2020) illustrates this point, as did *Items: Is Fashion Modern?* (2017), which included a substantial number of experimental designs. Both shows were curated by my colleague Paola Antonelli. The Young Architects Program was also important in providing young offices with an opportunity to explore experimental design approaches in the highly visible courtyard of MoMA PS1. ○

> MoMA's collecting practices seem to be balanced between acquiring objects because they're exceptional and acquiring them because they're ubiquitous. How do you and your colleagues address this balance? Is there a desired ratio of characteristics, or is it about finding moments where they intersect, as with Hector Guimard's entrance gate for the Paris Métro, for example?

This question directly relates to what we were discussing earlier. One could say that the very idea of "good design" is that design worthy of being in MoMA's collection can and should be exceptional and ubiquitous at the same time, so the two categories aren't necessarily opposed. The question of what enters the collection is an ongoing conversation guided by a great number of parameters. It could perhaps be said that the architecture collection was built using an authorial model that focused primarily on exceptional projects by exceptional individuals. Conversely, the design collection's historical raison d'être was to be a repository of standard designs—what Le Corbusier would have called "*objets-type*"—that had been honed to "perfection," often through a collective, sometimes anonymous effort.

Besides expanding on the logic and history of the collection, when I started at MoMA I also wanted to critically challenge these established methods of canonization from a contemporary perspective. In particular, I'm interested in challenging the Western-centric worldview that underlies our collection by looking at geographies that have historically been underrepresented. Moreover, we've also set ourselves an institution-wide strategic objective to work toward more of a gender balance and to better represent ethnic minorities. As we have become painfully aware, none of these issues have been adequately taken into account historically, but they present themselves with great urgency— and not just for reasons of "political correctness" but for the significance of many of these voices for contemporary cultural production and conversation.

We also want to build on the logic of the existing collection. One of its criteria is the exceptionality of things. When we're interested in an architect or a designer, we ask ourselves: What are the key projects and objects? How do they relate to the existing collection, and why should they be a part of it? Conversely, our *Humble Masterpieces* series, which was begun by my colleague Paola Antonelli, relates to MoMA's early efforts to collect examples of industrial design that have become

○
Davorin Savnik, ETA 85 Telephone, Iskra Department of Design, 1979.
Photograph by Thomas Griesel.
Image courtesy of The Museum of Modern Art.

ubiquitous. Both approaches remain valid and inform our decisions.

This dialectical approach was represented in *Toward a Concrete Utopia* as well. On the one hand, the show included many architectural drawings that were exceptional both as singular works of art and as representations of exceptional buildings; on the other hand, it also had a design gallery filled with mass-produced objects that were widely available in the Yugoslavian context, like the Iskra telephone, which is part of MoMA's collection. ○

> Does collecting mass-produced design objects work differently from other forms of collecting, or do they involve similar processes?

Industrial design is by definition based on reproduction and multiplication. Yet as much as collecting industrial design is about the reproducibility of the object, it's also about highlighting exceptional thinkers. Conversely, architecture isn't typically multiplied, except in a prefabricated system. Whether we're collecting industrial design or architectural objects, though, the processes aren't dissimilar except that we apply different categories for each of the disciplines to assess whether a work is worthy of being included in the collection. We also source the work in different ways: architectural drawings and models often come directly from the architects and their offices, while design is frequently sourced from the manufacturer. There's also not much of a market for architectural drawings—except in rare exceptions—whereas design objects are often featured in auctions and specialized galleries.

> MoMA holds a collection of architectural mock-ups and building fragments. As a curator, how do you work with full-scale pieces of a building compared to other forms of representation? What is the importance of the fragment in communicating to a broader audience?

The presentation of architectural fragments in the museum context provides an interesting challenge. Think, for example, of Hector Guimard's gate for the Paris Métro, which has been a beloved part of the museum's Sculpture Garden for many years and is easily recognizable to our visitors as a "transplant" across space and time. ○

The situation becomes a bit more complicated with objects that are more fragmentary and less

Hector Guimard, Entrance Gate to Paris Subway (Métropolitain) Station,
Paris, France, ca. 1900. Photograph by John Wronn.
Image courtesy of The Museum of Modern Art.

complete. There the challenge is to make sure that visitors understand they're seeing an actual piece of architecture, as opposed to a sculpture, for example. The museum expansion last fall gave us an opportunity to explore the possibilities of presenting an architectural fragment in a gallery context. For example, we wanted to show a section of the original curtain-wall facade of the United Nations building in New York City, a recent acquisition, for the first time in our galleries. ○   The question was; How do you introduce an object like this into a gallery without it appearing to be a sculpture? How do you make sure visitors understand the architectural and spatial dimensions of the building? Our solution was to place the "fragment"—a quite substantial one at that—in the center of the gallery, mounted on an almost invisible supporting frame, which gave the piece a sense of floating in space— very much akin to the idea of the curtain wall itself. Moreover, as the visitors enter the gallery, they encounter the facade fragment front and center and can catch, by looking through the glass, a glimpse of a movie we're projecting on the opposite wall, a clip from Jacques Tati's *Playtime*, which is a hilarious yet biting critique of architectural modernism and its appropriation by a dehumanizing corporate culture. In this way, we were able to spatialize a

COLLECTING AND DISPLAY

○
Installation view of the gallery "Architecture Systems" in the exhibition
Collection 1940s–1970s, The Museum of Modern Art, New York.
Photograph by Robert Gerhardt.
Image courtesy of The Museum of Modern Art.

critical discourse on late modernist architecture by combining a prototypical representative of late modernism with its subversion in contemporary cinema. I'm quite proud of this setup!

> In making these curatorial choices, are there ways of taking cues from previous MoMA shows and applying them to future ones? For example, the show *Buildings for Business and Government* at MoMA (1957) also included full-scale mock-ups of curtain-wall facades.

Buildings for Business and Government used photography to indicate how a fragment was part of an architectural context. This is a more literal way of doing it but certainly a straightforward and instructive one. The big challenge of an architectural exhibition is always that, as a general rule, you can show only representations as opposed to the "thing itself," which is a fundamental distinction from art exhibitions, where you generally don't want to deal with representations. The architectural fragment is an interesting exception to the rule, because it's indeed the object itself, or rather a part thereof. So the curator's task is to mark that ontological difference for the visitor; otherwise it becomes confusing.

To answer your question more directly: Yes we certainly mine the history of our exhibitions and the way our predecessors installed the galleries, and many established procedures have been very successful over time. At the same time, we're always interested in coming up with new ways of display that are relevant to and tailored toward the singular nature of each exhibition. In recent years we've started to include the moving image more often than before as a really useful medium to give audiences an understanding of what a space looks and feels like.

> You've written about the history of how photographs and other architectural representations have entered the MoMA collection, either through the Study Centers or as part of the collection. You distinguish between objects in the collection proper and those that belong to the archive. How do you determine whether a photograph should be included in the collection of the Department of Photography or the Department of Architecture and Design?

The photo collection in the Department of Architecture and Design originated out of the need to document buildings visually, and so, initially, these photographs were not thought of as having artistic value as such and were thus considered part of the study collection only. Over time, the department accumulated an impressive library of some 70,000 images, many of which were taken by important architectural photographers, such as Ezra Stoller or Julius Shulman. We've started to review these holdings in a push to promote some of these extraordinary works into the full collection and to make them more accessible online, but given the sheer size of this photo library, this will be an ambitious and time-consuming project. This reconsideration of the photo library is also indicative of an emerging understanding of "architectural photography" as a hybrid category between documentation and the artistic interpretation of a building. In recent years, our collection policies have changed, and we usually try to represent an individual building through a variety of media, including models, drawings, photographs, and film, all of which enter the (full) collection. In recent years we've also started to collect architectural photography by important authors irrespective of whether the buildings are represented in other mediums in the collection; I'm thinking, for example, of Walter Niedermayr's work for SANAA or that of Hélène Binet or Hans Danuser for Peter Zumthor. In addition to this, the Department of Photography collects photographs related to the built environment, but there the focus is on the artistic interpretation more than on the representational value; for instance, the work of Hiroshi Sugimoto. These boundaries are fluid of course, and in many instances overlap. In all of these instances, we're in conversation with our colleagues from the photo department to coordinate our efforts.

> It's interesting to reflect on this question of photography's role in the work of major architectural photographers of the twentieth century. For instance, with Ezra Stoller, there is a conflict between the desire to assign authorship and intentionality to the photographs and the fact that many of the photographs were commercially commissioned and were intended to be cropped or otherwise tailored for trade purposes.

That's precisely the dilemma of architectural photography. It's a strange intermediary between these two poles, but it's exactly the hybrid nature of architectural photography between artistic autonomy and document that makes it so interesting. I think Ezra Stoller's work is a great example that indicates it's possible to be both. I would even go so far as to say that successful architectural photography always includes both aspects. Interestingly, in the moment of their production, many of these photographs were not yet considered to have the authorial status that we assign to them today, and recent scholarship on this topic has helped us better understand the precarious definition of what architectural photography is.

> How does the idea of photography as artwork play out in an architectural context; for example, with Valentin Jeck's photographs you commissioned for *Toward a Concrete Utopia*? Have they entered the collection? Is it important to keep the original prints, or would you reprint them? How are they used?

The large blowups on view in *Toward a Concrete Utopia* were exhibition copies and were destroyed after the show closed. ○   In this case, we acquired a set of photographs in the form of digital data, which will allow us to reproduce these images for future exhibitions and displays in a format and medium that we find adequate, whether as another exhibition copy or as a digital image. We would of

○
Installation view of the exhibition *Toward a Concrete Utopia: Architecture in Yugoslavia, 1948–1980*, July 15, 2018 to January 13, 2019, The Museum of Modern Art, New York. Photograph by Martin Seck.
Image courtesy of The Museum of Modern Art.

course always discuss with the artist previously before making a decision on how a photo is going to be presented. In addition, we also acquired a smaller set of these photos in the form of prints, where everything, including the format, type of print, and paper quality, was defined by the artist's intentions.

> How do you limit bias to ensure that you are incorporating a diversity of viewpoints in deciding what to exhibit and what objects to acquire?

Choices are always biased, and we all work within our own realm of experience. While each of the curators in the department has their own set of interests, the historical and ongoing lack of a more diverse staff and the consequences of that for our activities and programs are a matter of ongoing conversation and debate. These conversations have only taken on more urgency over the last few years. As a department, we've set ourselves the strategic goal of challenging the implicit biases of our Euro-centric collection by paying more and sustained attention to architects and designers of color, to women artists, and to work from outside the Western world. I believe that our more recent exhibition program and acquisitions, our collection installations, and the exhibitions that are currently in planning speak to this effort. Besides *Toward a Concrete Utopia*, for example, our recent exhibitions include *Reconstructions: Architecture and Blackness in America* (2021), which gave space to African American architects in MoMA's galleries for the first time, and *The Project of Independence: Architectures of Decolonization in South Asia, 1947–1985* (2022). In each of these instances, the curatorial team was reinforced and supported by an advisory board of leading scholars in their respective fields, who have brought much-needed expertise and diversity to the table. I believe our generation of curators has a duty to address these implicit institutional biases and address our blind spots.

As someone who began as a historian and then became a museum curator, how has working in a curatorial capacity altered your research methodology?

As a scholar with an academic background, it was always important to me that I would be able to continue doing my research as a curator. I see curating as a form of research in public. That said, research in the museum is much more collaborative than it is in academia. For archival research, I can rely on a fantastic team of assistants who can help me, whereas in an academic environment I would usually have done work like that myself. On the other hand, the museum provides access and means to speak directly to architects and key protagonists. It's a truly great privilege that comes with this job.

I'm probably also more strategic in identifying my research projects now. I'm aware that whatever I do at the museum has visibility and an impact on architectural discourse that is likely greater than if I were a professor at a university. With this comes a sense of responsibility.

How does working at MoMA, a large institution with substantial resources, differ from working at a smaller institution?

For example, in our conversation with Mario Ballesteros, he described the smaller scale of his organization (Archivo Diseño y Arquitectura in Mexico City), which mounts at least three exhibitions a year, as a strength. How does MoMA's institutional scale affect your exhibition calendar or the process of developing your ideas?

The frequency of shows has to do with the ethos of MoMA as a research institution. As a scholar, I wouldn't be interested in working in an environment where I had to mount three shows annually, because that would by necessity have to be a somewhat superficial endeavor. Some curators are comfortable with that framework, but for me the research component is essential. It's impossible to curate a thoroughly researched show in six months, and consequently it would lead to a different way of working.

For sure, a large institution such as MoMA can feel a little slow, or inert. Often we can't respond as quickly to current concerns as we would like. However, within the expanded museum that we opened in the fall of 2019, the third-floor gallery and the new street-front gallery on the ground floor give the architecture and design department an opportunity to do things in a relatively short time-frame. We want to use that type of space for more nimble interventions where we can respond much more quickly to contemporary issues.

> You've mentioned a certain self-awareness of the visibility of your position at MoMA, knowing that thirty years from now, some-one might reference an exhibition catalog or quote from one of your lectures as a touchstone of how the architectural canon has progressed. How do you think about the double temporality of your exhibitions, between the shorter term of public con-sciousness and the longer-term effects within architectural discourse?

I'm aware of how MoMA has told the history of modern architecture and design, and a key driver of what I do now is how I want to situate myself within that history. My responsibility as a curator of the present is to evaluate and assess that history critically. That, I believe, is the challenge and primary task for every new generation of curators. That said, I see my work more as a continuation of the work of my immediate predecessor, rather than as a radical departure. For example, Barry Bergdoll's

*Latin America in Construction: Architecture 1955–
1980* (2015) served as a model for a more global
perspective of architectural history in the postwar period.

In general, the ambition of every exhibition
project is to speak in meaningful ways both to
the moment in which it's produced and to the
longer arc of history. As historians, we have an
obligation to continuously question and revisit
preconceived notions of how history has been
written and to be aware of the ways in which it
is socially constructed.

> *Toward a Concrete Utopia* was framed
> partly around the idea that the era and topic
> it covers have been relatively underrepre-
> sented in architectural discourse, at least
> in the United States. In both architecture
> and the arts the trend has been toward a
> more social, contextual approach to exhibi-
> tions: a focus on movements, geographies,
> or historical periods that have traditionally
> been marginalized or less visible. Do you see
> this as a shift away from more traditional,
> formal readings, or do these approaches
> mutually inform one another to expand the
> canonical history of architecture?

MARTINO STIERLI

I'm unsure whether the trend toward global art history, into which the Yugoslavia exhibition probably falls, is directly related to a more socially or politically driven approach. If you are asking whether formal resolution in art or architecture becomes less relevant in this kind of exhibition or research project, I do not think that is the case. I'm interested in how problems of architectural and urban space are resolved formally. However, I try to situate those questions within a larger socioeconomic and political context. *Toward a Concrete Utopia* was an investigation at the intersection of these poles in that it explored the ways in which architects, through their designs and buildings, were agents in the progressive transformation of a society. ○ Our current exhibition, *The Project of Independence*, is conceived in a similar way. Many of the spatial programs of those buildings speak to a larger societal vision that was shared by many of the architects.

I also don't believe that a consideration of things previously thought of as peripheral is a fetishization of the margins—indeed, a key notion we wanted to communicate was that the architecture of socialist Yugoslavia was anything but marginal, either for the architectural production of its time or from our present perspective. It isn't methodologically interesting or innovative in itself

○
Installation view of the exhibition *Toward a Concrete Utopia: Architecture in Yugoslavia, 1948–1980*, July 15, 2018 to January 13, 2019, The Museum of Modern Art, New York. Photograph by Martin Seck.
Image courtesy of The Museum of Modern Art.

to bring material histories from underrepresented or marginalized parts of the world into the conversation simply for the sake of novelty. I believe *Toward a Concrete Utopia* was successful in starting a conversation that went beyond that and led to the more fundamental question of how architecture can make a meaningful impact on society more broadly and how it can be an agent for change.

> You've described the curation of *Toward a Concrete Utopia* in terms of "double coding," the idea that signs are open to different interpretations depending on the frame of reference. How do these strategies of double coding appear in the exhibition?

In speaking of "double coding," I was making a point about differentiating the various media we were orchestrating to address different audiences. While many architectural drawings are stunning works of art in their own right, we have to acknowledge that the general audience often feels put off by drawings of a more technical nature; for example, a floor plan. They can feel inhibited— "Oh, it's an architectural drawing, and I don't understand it; it's too technical, and I can't read it." So the inclusion of plans is a more specific offering to a professional audience. Media such as video and photography, conversely, while also of interest to professionals, offer much more of an invitation for a general audience to access material they might otherwise not feel comfortable engaging with. So, for me, the ambition and the challenge of an architectural exhibition is to speak in two registers. The exhibition should speak in a professional and a popular voice at once, without losing intellectual rigor.

> MoMA's institutional scale is also reflected in the large number of objects that can be displayed in a given show. In *Toward a Concrete Utopia*, for example, roughly eight hundred objects were on display. While this quantity is presumably related to the desire to bring together different media to reach a wide variety of audiences, is there ever a risk of redundancy or overload in what is being shown? Can there be too much?

There can absolutely be too many objects. Editing is one of the most painful but also most essential activities in the entire curatorial process. For *Toward a Concrete Utopia*, we literally had to choose from among thousands of objects that could have been included. The dilemma is always between breadth and depth. Do you want to represent a building with ten gorgeous drawings, or do so even more comprehensively with photography and even film? Or do you limit yourself to two exceptional things and then have the space to show another building instead? In this case, we wanted the exhibition to be material driven. We scrutinized what was available and how we could use that material in the best possible way to build and support our narrative, which we organized in four large chapters. In that sense, there's a clear differentiation between the exhibition and the book. The book includes materials that may not be so visually stunning or useful for an exhibition but are important as historical artifacts. The exhibition is a medium in its own right; it's important to understand that and to make the best use of how meaning can be produced in a spatial display. You don't want oversaturation, because that leads to fatigue. *Toward a Concrete Utopia* covered about ten thousand square feet, and that, in my opinion, is about as big as you can go with an architecture exhibition without exhausting visitors—unless you build immersive spaces or spatial experiences that, by their very nature, are even more space-consuming.

> You have explained, as a scholar, how the typical outlet for that kind of research and production used to be the book, whereas now it takes place through exhibitions. Could you elaborate on how the book and the exhibition are different, or on how these are complementary?

The conceptualization of the Yugoslavia show wasn't driven by a bookish understanding of how to develop a narrative. It was materially driven and dealt with the question of how to communicate a set of narratives in an exhibition space, which is quite different from the communication of narratives in a text. Many aspects of the story that are important to understanding the material contextually—for example, the country's political history, the system of self-management through which Yugoslav economics worked, or the repercussions of that economic model on architecture culture through the Yugoslav competition system for projects—are difficult to represent in an exhibition because there's no direct visual material. The book is the better medium to discuss these theoretical perspectives. In an exhibition, you want to reduce your argument to a limited number of stringent points supported by visual material to bring across the message. The book is then a complementary tool to add nuance and context. I'm generally quite critical of architectural exhibitions that fail to distinguish between the inherent qualities of each of these mediums and that present complex arguments with long texts on panels that would be better presented in a book.

> How does the exhibition catalog fit into this dynamic?

Historically speaking, exhibition catalogs were often a direct record of what was on view; catalogs would include checklists of works shown, for example. While historically it was important for future scholars to be able to reconstruct what was on view, this information can now be stored and made accessible in different ways through digital platforms. This allows for the catalog to take on a new kind of autonomy with regard to the exhibition. For me, it's important that the catalog presents state-of-the-art research on a given topic that contributes to critical discourse while at the same time presenting a visually attractive and stimulating record of the exhibition. Consequently, my exhibition catalogs not only include essays by the curators but also give space to the voices of the leading scholars in a given field.

> In thinking about the audience for an exhibition, is it important to raise awareness of a particular cultural context or moment in architecture in order to ensure a particular reception?

I think it's difficult to anticipate a specific reception on the part of the audience, but in general I absolutely believe that explaining why a specific chapter or topic of architectural history is relevant for larger social, political, and cultural questions is helpful in raising interest and awareness. The question relates again to the matter of double coding: you want to make sure that an exhibition appeals to various audiences and constituencies that might visit in the larger context of a modern art museum and to provide a variety of entry points into any presentation of a complex issue so that it's accessible without losing texture and complexity.

> Is it important to localize awareness of an exhibition in the places where the architecture originated?

Absolutely. I think it's critical for architects and designers to see their work exhibited in a museum with a global presence such as MoMA and, conversely, to make sure that local audiences know about this presence. In the case of *Toward a Concrete Utopia*, we received an enormous amount of interest from within the former Yugoslavia. From the beginning, it was our hope that such an exhibition would help raise awareness of the legacy of modern architecture in the region and support initiatives for the preservation of these buildings, many of which are under threat.

Historically, many of MoMA's shows have traveled, and the museum has even had a separate department for circulating exhibitions. The history of these traveling exhibitions—their generation and dissemination—is part of why MoMA has had an outsized role in canon formation. Do you envision the Yugoslavia show or future exhibitions traveling to other institutions?

MoMA's traveling exhibition program originated as part of the soft-power and cultural politics of the United States at the time. Our understanding of the world and the role of the museum is a bit different today, but MoMA continues to collaborate with institutions elsewhere to present its exhibitions. In the more recent past, architecture exhibitions on the scale of *Toward a Concrete Utopia* have unfortunately rarely traveled, mainly for pragmatic reasons. They're undertakings of enormous complexity, including a large number of lenders and a variety of mediums, all of which make traveling very expensive. On the other hand, people are much more mobile today, and it's easier for them to travel. Moreover, with our modern means of communication, we have ways of making the contents of our exhibitions accessible online, even though these media cannot replace the actual spatial experience of an exhibition. The lockdown of the museum due to the COVID-19 pandemic has pushed the institution forward in thinking more strategically about how we can use our online platform to reach our global audience, and many of the initiatives started under these circumstances will expand. That said, in an ideal world our exhibitions would certainly travel to the places where the material originates, particularly as a way to highlight their significance and value for future preservation. This is a huge issue in particular with global postwar modernisms.

> The audience for a book is different from the audience for a museum. You have talked about the experience of people stumbling into an exhibition and encountering a subject they likely would not have seen before. In contrast, people are less likely to stumble upon a catalog, read it, and gain from it. Is there value in a traveling exhibition that has less to do with spatial experience and more to do with the knowledge that can be acquired from a chance encounter?

The "stumbling in" works only in large institutions like MoMA that have many exhibitions on view at any given time. In a museum dedicated to architecture, you would usually have only one large exhibition on view, and therefore only people with a preexisting interest in the topic would be likely to come. So the fact that MoMA has one of the most important collections of modern art in the world is actually a huge advantage and opportunity for us. I think this is true irrespective of whether an exhibition travels or not.

> There are inherent structural and temporal differences between the permanent record (the book) and the ephemeral experience (the exhibition). How do these two products relate to one another temporally?

What you are saying is absolutely right. Exhibitions are there for only a limited period of time, and once they're over it's very difficult or impossible to reassemble them again, even though reconstructions of important shows of the past have become more popular in recent years. The book, on the other hand, is there to stay and can contribute to discourse in the future in contexts we cannot even imagine from the perspective of the present. Needless to say, the legacy of an exhibition can be preserved in other ways too. At MoMA, every

○
Installation view of the exhibition *Italy: The New Domestic Landscape*,
May 26 to September 11, 1972, The Museum of Modern Art, New York.
Photograph by Leonardo LeGrand.
Image courtesy of The Museum of Modern Art.

exhibition now has its own web page and is amply documented with installation views, checklists, links to catalogs, and other resources. I believe these online offerings will be enormously helpful for future researchers. But there always remains the actual physical and spatial experience of visiting an exhibition, and I think it's precisely the relative ephemerality of exhibitions that in many instances has helped to build a kind of mystique around them: I'm always slightly envious, for example, when I hear other people speak vividly about seminal exhibitions such as *Information* or *Italy: The New Domestic Landscape*. ○   These accounts speak to the undiminished power of exhibitions even in our digital age. The COVID-induced lockdown has made the longing for actual physical encounters only more acute.

Martino Stierli is the Philip Johnson Chief Curator of Architecture and Design at the Museum of Modern Art (MoMA) in New York. The initial conversation on which this text is based took place in Houston in September 2018.

GIOVANNA BORASI

MUSEUM WORK AND MUSEUM PROBLEMS

GIOVANNA BORASI

> The Canadian Centre for Architecture
> (CCA) is one of the few architecture-specific
> museums in the world. Do you intend for
> the CCA's audience to be comprised mostly
> of architects, or are you trying to bring in
> a more unfamiliar public?

We're trying to bring in not just architects but also an unfamiliar public. We don't show architecture in an explicitly professional sense. So, if you want an update on the current status of architecture in the world, the CCA is not necessarily the place to get those answers. When we talk about architects still being our main public, I mean an "intellectual" (without sounding snobbish) architect, someone interested in going beyond questions of construction or tectonics.

I also don't think a definition of the general public exists anymore. Many museums are currently trying to define the public and the persona of their attendees. Ultimately, our interest is in a public unfamiliar with architecture but curious about discovering and engaging with other thematics.

> How do you go about reaching this "unfamiliar public"?

We work on how to convey particular ideas connected to architecture so that the general public can understand them. We do use traditional architectural artifacts such as models, drawings, diagrams, documents, notes, and correspondences. But one of the things we do differently is that we, as curators, also invent objects; for instance, the paper animals from the exhibition *Imperfect Health: The Medicalization of Architecture* (2011). In a room dedicated to epidemics, we wanted to convey the feeling of being surrounded by animals, which, while familiar, are often responsible for the spread of disease. We thought about how we could communicate these ideas differently, beyond just showing projects like MVRDV's Pig City (2001) or a drawing by Cedric Price from his Westpen project (1977–1979). Ultimately, those are still drawings by architects. I had seen Andy Byers's work with Isabella Rossellini on the short film series *Green Porno* (2008), which included paper animals, so we commissioned him to make three. We gave him dimensional references from Ernst Neufert's *Bauentwurfslehre* (*Architects' Data*, 1943), which is part of the CCA's collection. We have the first edition, and I think the scale of the animals was different at the time the book was published, because the cow Andy did at 1:1 scale is amusingly small compared to current cows. ○

GIOVANNA BORASI

Why are you so scared? We live in a health-obsessed society. Obesity is an epidemic. Is health an individual responsibility or a public concern? Do architectural types mirror the specialized needs of medicine? Urban environments pose ever-increasing challenges to our health. Is healthism our new religion? Do we all share the same ideas about health and illness? Desi... ...s heal damage from ... you live in a ... ...sed to risk

○
Installation view of the exhibition *Imperfect Health: The Medicalization of Architecture*, 2011, CCA. Photograph by Michel Legendre.
Image courtesy of the Canadian Centre for Architecture (CCA).

In the same exhibition we wanted to show some of the detoxifying plants used to remediate soil, so we 3D-printed whole sets of algae. They became a kind of physical and magical set of objects in the gallery. In that sense, a different way of responding to your question about the public is: How do you capture someone's attention and then encourage the person to read the story beyond what's represented? For our exhibition *Journeys: How Travelling Fruit, Ideas and Buildings Rearrange Our Environment* (2010), I decided not to include any direct representations of people. Instead, only animals and fruits were shown. The first story in the exhibition was about how a particular European law had, as a result of mass distribution, basically defined what the *right* cucumber is. The law outlines the ideal proportions and possible distortions of a cucumber, and it was translated into twenty-three languages. We represented this by having an ideal cucumber in the gallery. Then, throughout the summer, I asked my colleagues to bring in organic cucumbers of different shapes, and we produced a collection of photographs and provided anatomical readings of the vegetables similar to criminologist Cesare Lombroso's readings of human faces. The images of the cucumbers were framed and treated as traditional museum objects. The story was a way to

GIOVANNA BORASI

illustrate metaphorically how in our society we often put forward policies based on biased standards.

> How do you choose between creating new objects versus using more conventionally "authored" artifacts to convey curatorial ideas? What conceptual problems do you encounter in each case?

At times we've been criticized for our process. There's a line between being a curator and being an artist or an author who creates an object. For objects authored by others, we also have to consider the question of appropriation when we use a work to convey a reading that differs from the artist's intentions. For example, the CCA commissioned three photographers—Lee Friedlander, Robert Burley, and Geoffrey James—to photograph all of the parks designed by Frederick Law Olmsted over a particular eight-year period. In the end, the CCA acquired one thousand photographs of the Olmsted parks for its collection. We ended up using a series of Burley's Olmsted photographs in the exhibition and publication *Imperfect Health: The Medicalization of Architecture* (2011–2012) to make a point about green spaces in the city; namely, their ambiguity as what Olmsted called the "lungs of the city" but also as an abundant source of potential allergens for many residents. Maybe the photographer wasn't happy because we gave his photographs a meaning that wasn't the initial intention or within the author's scope. There's a kind of appropriation in making your own narrative using an artist's work. In that instance, we created a wall label where the discrepancy was clearly stated, similar to an editorial note in a book. In these situations, we use the author's original caption along with another that conveys the curator's voice, which might tell a completely different story. The distinction should be clear to the public.

> As a research institution, why does the CCA choose to engage an "unfamiliar public" with architecture rather than focusing on a disciplinary audience of people who are looking to expand their understanding of architecture on a different level?

An answer to that question involves many factors. First, our mission is to make architecture a public concern. That was the ethos Phyllis Lambert established when she founded the CCA. So we need to think beyond the architects. Our core public still comprises architects, intellectuals, critics,

policymakers, and people who work within the
fields of architecture and urbanism. But we advocate
for the idea that architecture should become a
concern for people not explicitly involved with the
discipline. This is connected to our belief that
architectural thinking leaves traces in many more
kinds of objects than the ones typically associated
with architectural practice. We're interested in architectural processes distinct from the model of the
imperious principal architect, ones that involve the
people whose environment is being changed, ones
that expand the definition of "doing architecture."

At the CCA we believe that "architecture" is
not just the building. We may lose some hard-core
architects who want our exhibitions to stay within
conventional disciplinary boundaries, but we
gain this other, larger public interested in design
or urban issues. When we did the exhibition
*The University Is Now on Air: Broadcasting Modern
Architecture* (2017), we had lots of visitors who were
interested in media studies and digital humanities.
○   With each project, we invite a part of the
public that might not otherwise engage with us.

In your exhibition *Besides, History: Go
Hasegawa, Kersten Geers, David Van
Severen* (2017), the installations were

○
Installation view of the exhibition *The University Is Now on Air: Broadcasting Modern Architecture*, 2017, CCA. Photograph by Matthieu Brouillard. Image courtesy of the Canadian Centre for Architecture (CCA).

immersive, with little explanatory wall text. Some of the content was difficult to understand, even for trained architects, while other parts were experienced more viscerally. How do you negotiate these different modes of understanding through the display of an exhibition? Does removing text narrow or widen the gap?

Not having an educational department but rather a public department, we don't have fixed standards but rather an array of tools that the curator or the curatorial team can advocate using. Some curators think they have to explain everything; they take you by the hand. For example, for our exhibition *Architecture in Uniform* (2011) with Jean-Louis Cohen, we calculated that, if you read all of the text in the galleries, you'd need six hours and twenty-three minutes to view the entire show.

I think that, as curators in the discipline of architecture, we should learn from curation at large. For me, it's okay go to an art show and just have a visual impression of things. You might not understand the artist's intentions or even what the topic is, but you can have a first impression. It's like flipping a book and just looking at the images; you can get a sense of what the thing is about. For me, that visual impression is fundamental. You have to assume a visitor who won't take a guided tour, won't want to read any of the wall texts, and yet will still want to grasp something from your show. You have to impart some understanding solely through visual terms. This comes back to the idea of establishing hierarchies and communicating to visitors what the key objects in the gallery are.

The way we work is through curatorial sequence. Curators are often historians—well equipped to focus on the argument and what they want to convey through objects but less equipped to communicate these ideas in space. Our process begins with a drawing that identifies the first object you want visitors to see in a space and the narrative you intend to build. It's a storyboard, a sequence of images in scale as a representation of the real objects. When you enter a gallery, for example, objects displayed horizontally aren't the first thing you see. So, if it's an exhibition based on the contents of a book—and many of our curators have relied on books—the book itself won't be the first thing you see.

As a curator, I build my narrative through the physical reality of the objects: one might be tiny, one horizontal, and another cannot be exposed to light. This process is different from designing a book, where you can scale up and expand the images or create an aura around an image using the surrounding white space. In a book, you know the direction in which people will read, but in space, you can't simply place the first object next to the path you think people will take. The sequence isn't prescribed.

Text can be used as another appendage in creating a curatorial sequence. For example, if I have a single caption for a group of objects, I'm suggesting those objects should be read together. Even the decision of whether to include a lot of text or no text impacts the reading of the narrative and the perceived importance of these objects. Translating this editing process into space is very interesting to me.

As we were developing and launching *Besides, History*, I worried that people wouldn't understand the overall thesis, about the relationship contemporary architects have with certain historical figures or moments in history. The exhibition was conceived as a dialogue between two contemporary practices (Go Hasegawa and OFFICE Kersten Geers David Van Severen) and as an illustration of their reckoning with history. To do this, we showed their projects in relation to their possibly desired connections with the past. In one room were models of projects, with no drawings and no explanation.

In the next room was a construction at 1:1 scale.
○   One of the galleries was filled solely with
plans, carefully chosen so that, for example, a
Renaissance plan by Andrea Palladio was juxta-
posed with a contemporary plan by OFFICE. The
audience may not be familiar with Palladio or
OFFICE, but they can still have a visual understanding about how to read a plan and how the
two practices are connected through their use
of this representational format. Now, I'd thought
it would be tied too strongly to a disciplinary
discourse and would require a lot of explanation,
but the show turned out to be the one where
this sort of explanation was least needed. The
content was presented in a way that conveyed a
clear visual impression.

I saw this also in the first show we did in
the same series of exhibitions by architects,
Environment: Approaches for Tomorrow (2006–2007),
with Philippe Rahm and Gilles Clément, as well as
in *Some Ideas on Living in London and Tokyo* (2008),
by Stephen Taylor and Ryue Nishizawa. In both the
Besides, History show and the *Some Ideas on Living
in London and Tokyo* show, the displays and the
content were entangled. You would be in a room
with a model, and you wouldn't look at the model as
a model—you were *inside* the model. To me, that's a

○
Installation views of the exhibition *Besides, History: Go Hasegawa, Kersten Geers, David Van Severen*, 2017, CCA. Photograph by Matthieu Brouillard. Image courtesy of the Canadian Centre for Architecture (CCA).

very interesting take. You see lots of installations by architects that want to be art pieces—they're not as good as artworks but also are not architecture. In *Besides, History*, we were able to avoid that. You were actually inside the content, physically experiencing it, without the work becoming an art installation piece.

GIOVANNA BORASI

> In a research institution where primary material can be anything from a model to an airplane ticket, how do you filter your collections to create narratives? Do the CCA's collections offer more curatorial opportunities compared to traditional hierarchies of display between materials that have often been more valued in a gallery context, like models, and what might otherwise be considered less significant material?

The acquisition policy at the CCA makes clear that material must facilitate and stimulate research. In that sense, our policy is very different from that of an institution like MoMA, which can acquire works for their visual and exhibition potential. Our ethos makes the life of the curator, and of the researcher, complicated. With an archive, you can get thousands of boxes of stuff that's not particularly interesting visually or otherwise. We have a lot of redundancy, which I actually like and would never seek to reduce, because you can read meaning in repetition. If you look into the archive of Cedric Price, for example, you might find one hundred copies of the same document. You could leave out the copies and just keep the original, but if something was photocopied that many times, it must have been crucial. If the archive is for research, we need to maintain these possibilities for reading the material.

We often discuss different acquisition policies with the International Confederation of Architectural Museums (ICAM), of which the CCA is a member institution. For example, I remember discussions around this issue of redundancy with Barry Bergdoll. He would argue that at MoMA it's the curator's role to select five key drawings for a project, and those are what the audience then sees. In contrast, I would want to acquire every version of a project. The various versions have equal value in terms of information, even if as objects they might not have the same kind of visual interest or monetary value.

The archive can be deployed as primary material in other ways. In our exhibition *The Other Architect* (2015), I examined alternative working methods of architectural practice through various types of materials, including budgets, mission statements, meeting minutes, organization charts, and other archival documents. ○   To substantiate the idea of the intellectual contribution of the architect to the discipline, being able to dive into an archive with its large and complex body was essential. By expanding the scope of what we examine, we can broaden our understanding of what architecture is.

GIOVANNA BORASI

○
Installation view of the exhibition *The Other Architect*, 2015, CCA.
Photograph by Matthieu Brouillard.
Image courtesy of the Canadian Centre for Architecture (CCA).

Not filtering incoming acquisitions, as we might if we were interested only in what was visually striking, allows for this broadening.

> How do these issues of collecting and display relate to the questions of authorship you described earlier, from the materials you acquire to the new objects you introduce?

The museum has had to adapt to this process and philosophy where we introduce all these unusual objects into the collection or else we create objects with a weird status, like the paper animals in *Imperfect Health* or the "wrong" cucumbers in *Journeys*. If I want the photographs of these cucumbers to enter the collection, questions then arise about authorship. The simple museum data organization that states the author who created the work, its title, who photographed the work, and who has the copyright is then difficult to define. Museums still organize information based on the model of a traditional art collection where you have an object and, if you don't know the author, it's listed with an "unknown." We now have a kind of escape from this strict system in our institutional archive. But we also still have many hybrid objects that we don't know exactly how to categorize within the collection.

In our exhibitions we clearly communicate what's original and what's not. We're not interested in tricking visitors with a reproduction or representation of a work. Sometimes in museums an object is labeled as an "exhibition print" but is framed as it would be for an original print. At the CCA we tend to clearly distinguish the original from the reproduction.

Sometimes we also exaggerate the value of an object through the display. For example, for the exhibition *Actions: What You Can Do With the City* (2008–2009), we borrowed a pair of shoes from a fourteen-year-old and displayed them in a kind of vitrine, as if they were in a natural history museum.
○   When we put them in this setting—illuminated, with velvet tissue underneath, surrounded by glass— the shoes suddenly became precious design objects. This is a kind of irony that we've explored with this type of presentation.

Do you see immersion as an important factor in an exhibition?

The best learning experience I had with an exhibition was working with the conceptual artist Martin

○
Installation view of the exhibition *Actions: What You Can Do With the City*, 2008 to 2009, CCA. Photograph by Michel Legendre.
Image courtesy of the Canadian Centre for Architecture (CCA).

Beck for the setup of *Journeys*. Beck compared the exhibition to a movie, where you want the viewer to cry at one point and feel suspense or surprise at another. We achieved this through what we called "emotional objects." We started to map out the exhibition in two ways: a dry plan with the curatorial sequence, showing my idea of how things should be seen, and another drawing representing the idea of emotional objects as anchors. As a result, the show had no "down" moments. The visitor's emotions were held in constant tension, which allowed us to maintain the attention span of a broad public.

As curators, we must deal with the public and the realities of how we all live now. How often are you in a gallery without using your phone or doing something else? The idea that you are fully there and that the artifact on display is the only thing you focus on isn't realistic anymore. It's especially important nowadays to organize an exhibition so as to create visual curiosity about the next step. The narrative is about not only the content but also the time and the rhythm in which you experience things.

> Is an immersive experience primarily tied to the physical space of an exhibition, or can a similar experience be produced through digital or written formats?

Structuring an exhibition is not so different from structuring an editorial piece. You have a beginning, a narrative, and an end. You always also try to challenge that format. In a written piece, you can skip chapters, but in a physical space you need a spatial sequence and narrative. The main difference, however, is that in an exhibition you can talk only about what you show, while in a book you can reference an object in the text or reproduce an image of it.

As a curator, you must be conscious about how you intend to direct visitors inside the exhibition space and where you want people to focus their attention. You must establish hierarchies. A person comes into a space with an immediate sense of what the most important piece is; sometimes it's tiny, so this isn't necessarily a question of scale. People have, for example, a tremendous attraction to digital works. If you place a film, a sculpture, and a drawing in a room, visitors will first watch the video, then look at the three-dimensional objects, and then maybe examine a drawing or read the text. In dealing with architectural objects or the surrogates we work with to represent architecture— the objects we invent or recreate—you have to play with these ideas about hierarchy, narrative, and sequence.

GIOVANNA BORASI

> How do you approach the increasing inclusion of digitally created work in your collections, something you began exploring with the *Archaeology of the Digital* (2013) exhibition?

The digital has its own character. When we began to access natively digital materials for our collections, we began asking ourselves questions not only about their presentation in an exhibition but also about how a scholar would look at them. We had done something similar in the earlier show curated by Lev Bratishenko, *404 ERROR: The object is not online* (2010–2011). It explored the idea of loss— for example, of scale or context—when transferring physical objects in the CCA collection to a digital format. The most published object in the CCA collection is a tiny drawing of the Fun Palace by Cedric Price. I think a lot of people publish it without understanding that it's actually a photograph of a drawing that he then drew on. We have a book in our collection by A.V. Narasimha Murthi and B.K. Gururaja Rao, *Rangavalli: Recent Researches in Indology* (1983), that contains spices, so when you open it you get this sensory experience that is evocative of India. If you just put a photo of it on the web, you would never understand this.

404 ERROR was about a kind of digital cunning in how you transfer a real object into the digital realm or place a digital-born object into physical space. The exhibition included a computer with AutoCAD drawings by Peter Eisenman's office. This created an interesting problem: a visitor who was AutoCAD savvy could potentially change Eisenman's drawings. On the other hand, the moment you put the drawing online you need to publish it as a PDF, which changes the way the content is displayed. The work we're trying to do now—made possible through a collaboration with the American Institute of Architects, who gave us their archival copies of old softwares—is meant to give us the ability to show a digital drawing in the right environment, but as a "read-only," so researchers can see a work in AutoCAD 7 or Photoshop 2 as it would have been in its original medium.

A difficulty with representing the digital is finding ways to encourage people to interact with these works. With *Archaeology of the Digital*, we saw that visitors didn't generally interact with the arrangement of computers in the show. People would see an AutoCAD screen on a computer and just pass to the next object. We understood that this wasn't the ideal way of showing these digital drawings either, so instead, we made a fly-through. That kind of display produced another problem for the collection because it was no longer the original drawing but a new 3D representation that we had created from the original. It was an interesting show because we were testing these ways of exhibiting digital material to the public. Now that we've done more digital projects, maybe we would do it differently.

> How does the growing presence of natively digital work in the CCA's archives affect the relationship between what is collected and what can be exhibited?

You're touching on a very good point. For instance, at the CCA we have the archive of Foreign Office Architects, and just the portion that contains their Yokohama International Port Terminal project includes something like ten thousand section drawings of the building. You could make all the material accessible and allow the visitor to sort through it, or you could start to treat the digital as if it were a traditional collection in which you select specific drawings because they reveal something critical. It's challenging because of the size of the archive; you can get lost in the metadata of a project. That's why many institutions refuse to store all representations or versions of a work. Today we have a much more consistent method of acquiring digital materials. It's a learning process, though.

> *Archaeology of the Digital* was a highly disciplinary exhibition, not only because you were showing disciplinary objects like architectural plans and sections, but also because so much of it was about having to explain or reconstruct the processes of architectural production—a task made more daunting still by the shifts in process that occurred with the advent of digital tools. How does the need to explain discipline-specific processes mesh with the interest in engaging both an architectural audience and a public that's unfamiliar with archi-tectural production? Does a show like *Archaeology of the Digital* cater to one audience over the other in contrast to a show like *Besides, History*, with its notion of letting architecture speak for itself without additional layers of communication?

I think the beauty of *Archaeology of the Digital* is that it was a long-term project. It had three chapters presented in three exhibitions, and through them there were twenty-five projects that we acquired for our collection. The materials for these projects have virtues that the general public won't be as interested in because they don't explain the projects in such a way that you could envision a finished building. In addition to the archival material acquired during the *Archaeology of the Digital* project, the collection also includes other early digital material; for example, a very nice inkjet print (and an early example of a digital drawing) of Arata Isozaki's Tokyo City Hall project from 1986. ○   Because the quality of printing has since improved so much, the print now mainly seems to provide information (besides the content) about the history of digital capabilities and how architectural representation and media have changed. Our eyes are used to a different digital output these days, and so some things are difficult for a public to see beauty or value in if they're not read through the lens of archaeology.

In that sense, we felt it was important for the CCA to attend to these sorts of early digital projects and position them carefully. We felt a sense of pressure. If we didn't work on collecting these materials, this part of the history of architecture and early digital representation would be lost. We would never be able to reopen and look at these drawings. Many architects just send us their hard

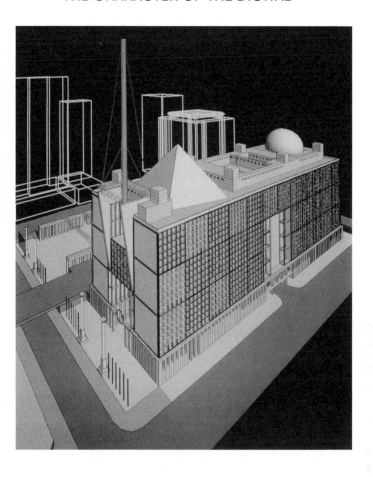

○
Bird's-eye view from the northwest for the Tokyo City Hall competition entry. Inkjet print, Arata Isozaki and Associates, 1986. © Arata Isozaki. Image courtesy of the Canadian Centre for Architecture (CCA).

drive, not knowing what's on it or if we'll even be able to open it. It's not that we "save" the works, but we do feel a pressure to keep them. For the discipline of architecture, those artifacts hold a part of the story that isn't always preserved.

> So much of the *Archaeology of the Digital* project was about the self-referentiality of an institution having to reflect on its own collection procedures. Do you see that self-referentiality as part of the broader idea of the CCA as a research institution, or is it an issue specific to the nature of collecting and displaying the digital?

Among the first architectural archives that the CCA acquired was Peter Eisenman's. He had boxes of digital material that were initially neglected because we privileged the paper material at that time. In previous acquisitions that had a digital component, the physical and digital works had always been considered separately. Thinking about how we process digital versus physical works led to a deep reflection on what the institution is and its responsibility in handling digital archives. What does scholarship mean now that you're looking at this data? People are now looking at the metadata—

the code. I don't even know what they're discovering there, but it's what they're looking at now.

For example, when we did the exhibition *Industrial Architecture: Ábalos & Herreros* (2015), the architects who were guest curators of the show, OFFICE Kersten Geers David Van Severen, were uninterested in the paper material and wanted to look only at the digital collection of Ábalos & Herreros. I didn't expect that from them. They looked at the firm's digital files as if they were the core of the work—where you would see the building itself—without the communication pieces from the office. This is also an important framing, because otherwise you'll always have drawings that show how the office presented the project. I hadn't thought about this previously, but by going directly into the AutoCAD files you suddenly had the design and only the design.

Ábalos & Herreros went digital in the 1990s, and the files were basic AutoCAD drawings. What OFFICE liked about using the digital component was that we could decide what to print. You could start to see plans and elevations as part of a recurring idea within Ábalos & Herreros's practice. The digital files allowed us some curatorial freedom because we could also print them in the format we wanted. We could decide to print everything at the same scale, or certain buildings at 1:10 scale, others at 1:50, and so on. With every exhibition, you look at the collection differently: either as a set of things you don't change at all, or as things you can start to play with.

> Beyond changes in architectural represen-
> tation, digital archives also change how we
> look at communication, labor, and other
> aspects of the bureaucracy of work. A paper
> archive, for example, might only include one
> side of a person's written correspondence,
> or an ink drawing that was so laborious that
> only one was made. How does the nature
> of digital storage change how we look at
> architectural production?

With digital platforms we get the full email corre-
spondence—both ends of the conversation. Of course, not everybody keeps everything. We've also received hard drives that contain divorce papers or bills for nannies and other sensitive information. We've had to return a lot of digital content that we didn't really want to have in the archive.

We have a fascinating forensic process for our digital collections. On the CCA website our digital archivists explain how to access a digital archive. Forensic software called Archivematica scans and divides the data into file types, unreadable material, viruses, and so on. Because it maps the data by file type, not content, things are described only in terms of format and size. Finding the love letters in a paper archive is much easier. With the digital, we're dealing with millions of gigabytes. For instance, when Greg Lynn donated his archive to the CCA, it was bigger than all of the digital archives we received during the previous forty years. So we have a massive storage problem. In the process of sorting through Lynn's archive, I'm sure we'll find surprises.

The other thing to consider is that many important conversations don't take place over email. For instance, the former president of the Venice Biennale, Paolo Baratta, came to see our archives because he wanted to organize an institutional archive of the history of the Biennale. For the early Biennales, they have a lot of correspondence discussing the ideas of the curators, and so on. For the later ones, though, he has only his WhatsApp messages, where Rem Koolhaas tells him, "Let's talk at the bar." A conversation like that has no interesting content; it's just a text message.

We have to consider other questions too. If you acquire the archive of an office, do you get the office's email? What or who constitutes "the office?" Does it include personal email accounts? And what do you do if it's a living person? Do they give up their email, or will we get their email feed forever? And what about social media? It's really terrible!

PUBLISHING FORMATS

In addition to its exploration of the digital in exhibitions and publications, the CCA maintains an extremely robust print publication program. Can you talk about the differences between these platforms and particularly how you choose whether to publish in a print or digital format?

The publication follows the logic of the exhibition. There's pressure to publish everything digitally, but I think we should do that only when it makes sense for the content. *Archaeology of the Digital* was the right project for us to start the process of digital publication; we've since done twenty-five e-publications. With something like a 3D drawing from Frank Gehry's office, instead of having a screenshot of a monitor as you might in a print publication, in an e-publication we can show the drawing as it would have behaved or appeared in the environment in which it was produced— or at least we can simulate or emulate that environment as much as possible. It's not yet possible to embed an AutoCAD or a Rhino file, but you can have a video of the drawing. To me, it was significant to have a digital form of publication that could reflect the original character of the source material.

GIOVANNA BORASI

Since 2018, we've been working with Andrew Witt at the Harvard Graduate School of Design on Studies in the Design Laboratory, a series of three e-publications on the intersection of design and science that describes architectural engagements with digital media. But paper books are still more important for us. I don't know how to continue this strategy of digital publications if the content isn't related to digital material. Our intention is to move more in the direction of podcasts or producing movies; that is, digital outputs that aren't books.

> You mentioned that the publication follows the logic of the exhibition and that print remains the primary format of the CCA's publications. What's the current strategy for the CCA's print publications?

We have thematic books, manifesto books, and more archival books, like *The Other Architect*. We've devised a process with Albert Ferré, our director of publications, in which we ask first, "What is the character of a CCA publication?" There has to be a visual narrative; you must be able to understand the content without reading it. Images are key. You might have toys, a book, or a drawing, but you must include a variety of materials that reflect the diversity and potency of the CCA collection and its research emphasis.

Each type of book has its own format. An archival publication might have a certain format because we want to publish materials at 1:1; a manifesto might have another format, and books that produce a reflection on the institution, another. We also change publishers for each book because we think there's a right publisher for each topic. For something that should have a larger presence in museum bookstores, we might work with certain publishers; for something we'd like to see in libraries all over the world, we might work with others. For each public we hope to reach, there's a different publishing strategy.

We've also started developing books for kids. We published one children's book by MOS for which they did all of the drawings. It tells the story of a family searching for a house to buy, with MOS's partners, Michael Meredith and Hilary Sample, as the parents. ○   The family visits a series of canonical houses—including, for instance, one by Peter Eisenman—and Hilary and the kids make comments: "Why is it so white?" "I don't understand that square," et cetera. Through the narrative of buying a house, you're introduced to the architectural history of modern houses. We're now working

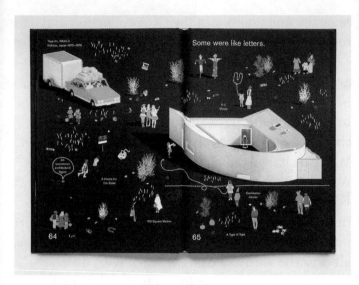

○
Michael Meredith and Hilary Sample, *Houses for Sale* (Montreal: Canadian Centre for Architecture; Mantua: Corraini Edizione, 2019).
Image courtesy of the Canadian Centre for Architecture (CCA).

on a new book with Paulo Tavares about forests in Amazonia, seen through the eyes of Indigenous people. The idea is to frame architectural and environmental problems for a young generation.

Our aim is to publish even more. I'd love to start publishing things that aren't necessarily initiated by the CCA but that we think are important to support or embrace as a contribution to architectural history or to the societal role of architecture at large.

How have these initiatives affected the scope and speed of the CCA's publishing program?

I thought it was important for the CCA to speed up its book production, so we started a series called Single as a reflection of other ways we consume content (think: buying one song instead of the whole album). Rather than a book that has twenty authors and an extensive narrative that takes two years to produce, each publication in the Single series is by one author and about one object or one event. These publications can emerge much more directly from the archive as a kind of raw material. For instance, the first volume in the series, by Stefano Graziani, is about his experience of finding Gordon Matta-Clark's personal library in the CCA collection. The Single volumes are about presenting the archival material as it is, getting it out, and then letting people use it as material with which to do something else.

The other component of our editorial production is our website. The CCA is a strange institution in that all of our communication is done not by a communications department but by the publications department—by an editor rather than by a public relations person.

I strongly believe that you achieve a certain result only by looking into the process. Putting intelligence into the process informs the final product—as does the selection of who works on the product. The scale of the CCA is such that we can work a lot on how we do things, much more so than other museums, where each department has separate responsibilities.

FROM CURATION TO RESEARCH

This conversation started before you became director of the CCA. Your purview now includes the CCA's Research Centre, whose work has run in parallel with its curatorial and publishing programs. How is the work of the Research Centre related to the CCA's exhibitions, and how do you see this relationship evolving?

To be precise, in my previous role of chief curator here at the CCA, I already had the responsibility of overseeing the research direction strategy and of giving meaning to all the ways we define the act of searching and researching at our institution. I also interpreted my role as chief curator to be an opportunity to make our four content areas (exhibitions and public programs, collection, publications, and research) work in an interrelated and interconnected way. Somehow all these areas of the institution conduct research. Understanding this, I saw a new opportunity: each time we decided on a topic of interest, we had the freedom to determine the preferred path to explore that topic. Do we start with a curatorial exploration? Do we build a network of scholars (especially helpful if internal expertise is lacking) and initiate a research project? Or do we start an editorial project? Each sequence or hierarchy of exploration would produce a very different output. For Centring Africa, for example, the CCA's fourth Mellon Multidisciplinary Research Project, conducted through the Research Centre starting in 2019, we worked with scholars in Africa or connected to the African diaspora to build a network of people and expertise—rather than launching ourselves into making a show. Several forms of work have come out of this—mainly published articles that explore the subject matter made accessible through these relationships. Other phases and projects will come after. This mode of working, where we start with relationships and areas of focus before deciding on a presentational form, will continue.

Meanwhile, new programs like our virtual fellowship were born of necessity during COVID-19, but they can give amazing access to scholars around the world. Notwithstanding what we lose when we can't experience things in person (and the technical challenges that have to be worked out), many people have come to appreciate the value of participating in culture remotely. We also have fellowships dedicated to Indigenous studies in order to support overlooked areas of knowledge and encourage expertise and interest in this field. Further, we are developing joint programs with other research institutes. We're starting with the Window Research Institute in Tokyo to explore the relationship between light, the environment, and architecture. We're also working on a new website, to be launched in 2023—the notion of access and shared knowledge will be its distinguishing character.

> The Research Centre's initiatives include the Multidisciplinary Research Program, whose recent topics have echoed broader disciplinary reckonings in architecture with urgent social issues such as climate change and environmental justice (Architecture and/for the Environment, 2017 to 2019), re-centering marginalized histories and geographies (Centring Africa: Postcolonial Perspectives on Architecture, 2019 to 2021), and digital media and social identity (The Digital Now: Architecture and Intersectionality, 2020 to 2022). How can research and exhibitions contribute to these forms of cultural reckoning, and how do you envision the CCA's role in these processes?

Such multidisciplinary projects have been and are fundamental contributions to these urgent discourses. Their beauty consists in the idea that scholars are in dialogue not only with one another but also with the CCA as an institution and with the public. In this way, the shift has been away from an individual scholar working on a subject and toward a community sharing both among themselves and well beyond their circle. This work has effects that range beyond academia and the discipline itself. Different modalities like these—be it a joint research program or an exhibition—are tools to tackle important contemporary issues. Architecture shouldn't be isolated from its context and looked at as if separate from the culture (social, economic, political) that produces it. So I might have an agenda—a bit activist, if you want—based on the belief that an institution like the CCA simply needs to take on the questions that society poses today.

> How do you ensure that the CCA's research and exhibition programs incorporate a diversity of viewpoints when you're deciding what's necessary today to study, discuss, display, or acquire?

The CCA has always been an international center trying to speak about fundamental ideas in architecture, regardless of where they come from. This means that, unlike many museums and cultural centers, we aren't tethered to one part of the world or one period of history. At the same time, the CCA isn't an encyclopedic museum and never aspired to be. Nevertheless, the CCA has in the past privileged a Western point of view both in its determination of what and where these moments were and in our way of looking at them. Today we are initiating many projects that challenge and move away from these tendencies.

c/o, for instance, is a program we started a few years ago wherein a curator in another geographic area points us to their perspectives on issues or questions that might not be understood as fundamental through our way of reading the world. For example, the series of publications Meanwhile in Japan, by Kayoko Ota (c/o Tokyo)—a response to Sylvia Lavin's reading of the postmodern period in North America, as reflected in her CCA exhibition *Architecture Itself and Other Postmodernist Myths* (2019)—offers a completely different way of looking at the same period in another geographic and cultural context.

Another new initiative that centers other perspectives is Find and Tell Elsewhere, which supports scholars to work with materials not held at the CCA. ○ This is an inversion of our Find and Tell program, in which we invite a scholar

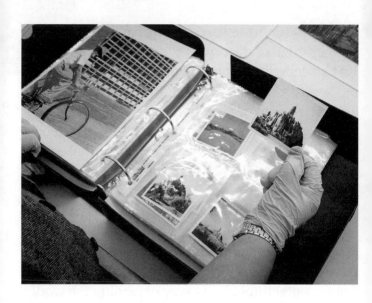

○
Sangeeta Bagga, Find and Tell. Research activities, CCA, 2019.
Photograph by Matthieu Brouillard.
Image courtesy of the Canadian Centre for Architecture (CCA).

from outside the CCA to come study specific material in our collection. Currently, we're working with African and Africanist scholars to bring attention to important but hard-to-access archives on the African continent and to support research, digitization, and dissemination of these important bodies of work. The material will be uploaded to Wikimedia (to ensure its distinction from the CCA collection) so it can be used and interpreted by the many voices we don't control, that speak in different languages, and that collectively represent a broad and complex knowledge. In this way, thanks to the digital world we live in, our role as a collecting museum shifts into the role of an instigator of research on areas we think are overlooked.

Giovanna Borasi is Director of the Canadian Centre for Architecture (CCA) in Montreal. The initial conversation on which this text is based took place in Houston in October 2018, when she was still serving in her role as Chief Curator at the CCA.

ANA MILJAČKI

TENDING TO DISCOURSE

ANA MILJAČKI

> In 2018 you launched the Critical Broad-
> casting Lab at the Massachusetts Institute
> of Technology (MIT), which you describe
> on the Lab's website as a platform for the
> production of discursive interventions in
> architecture culture, particularly through
> architectural exhibitions. What does the
> Lab do, who is involved, and how does its
> position in an academic institution enable
> the kinds of curatorial work you see as key
> to its mission?

The Critical Broadcasting Lab's key objectives are
to cultivate, seed, and multiply awareness about
the media economies we inhabit and, even more
important, the myriad contemporary and historical
entanglements of architecture and politics. By
politics I mean a broad constellation of issues that
involve the flows of global capital, labor, and
material, the climate crisis, the way the discipline
and individual architects conceptualize the subjects
for whom they design, the status of the object of
architecture in culture and in academia, the value
placed on authorship, the mechanisms used to
extract value from and with architecture, and so
on. All types of broadcasts—including exhibitions—
have a place in these constellations of political

issues, but for the Critical Broadcasting Lab, exhibitions are also tools by which to probe, represent, and mirror specific topics or circumstances so they can be further discussed and understood.

It matters that the Critical Broadcasting Lab's home is in academia rather than in a museum or other curatorial setting. Its role at MIT is pedagogical, providing a space of reflection that is collectively shared and shaped and that is carved out of the time normally dedicated to the elements of architectural education. It teaches the tools necessary to produce the distance needed for a critical understanding of complexity, nuance, and implication. Because the Lab exists in academia, its curatorial and broadcasting products aren't indebted to special interests, as they would be in many other situations and venues. Its curatorial and broadcasting projects are unsolicited and thus motivated by the urgencies felt by those who participate in them. The Critical Broadcasting Lab provides a space for political thinking and criticality that is open-ended toward aesthetic and critical outcomes that may be at a certain distance from architecture.

What are the key curatorial initiatives that the Lab has undertaken in the institutional context of MIT?

ANA MILJAČKI

Agit Arch Experiments (2018) was one of the first
ways the Critical Broadcasting Lab intervened
pedagogically in the context of MIT. Over three
weekends we conducted three workshops, each on
a different topic. ○   The first was "Dimensions of
Citizenship," which engaged Ann Lui, Mimi Zeiger,
and Niall Atkinson—the curators of the U.S. Pavilion
at the Venice Biennale in 2018—in order to take on
some of the topics they were outlining and expand
them through the interests of the workshop participants. The second workshop was "(Hacking) Click
Bait Politics," which focused on responding to the
media's sensationalizing of political topics, their
hashtagging and circulation through various modes
of communication. We wondered how we might
respond to those modes of producing political
narratives, whether we could identify and inject
counternarratives or new narratives into the flow.
We hoped to learn from the way clickbaiting
worked but also to irrigate the field with other
conversations and values. We worked with graphic
designer Luke Bulman to produce a series of non-
narrative books to which each student contributed
sixty-five images, which we then put together,
on topics ranging from border crossings to the
technological landscape to ruins to kinship. The
idea was to begin to tell stories that are somewhat

TENDING TO DISCOURSE

○
"Dimensions of Citizenship," event with Mimi Zeiger and Ann Lui held as part of *Agit Arch Experiments*, October 12 to 14, 2018, Massachusetts Institute of Technology (MIT), Cambridge (top).
"(Hacking) Click Bait Politics," event held as part of *Agit Arch Experiments*, November 2 to 4, 2018, MIT, Cambridge (bottom).
Images courtesy of the Critical Broadcasting Lab.

ambiguous but still elicit responses from those who engage with them.

The final workshop revolved around the topic of "Populism (and/with/in Architecture)." We examined architectural and other cultural artifacts that deal with the production of populist narratives, the aesthetic elements that make up the imaginary world of populist America. In each workshop we staged a public event with guests followed by two intensive days over the rest of the weekend for producing work and discussing it with our interlocutors. For the final event of the *Agit Arch Experiments* we created *Agit Arch Outpost*, a test exhibition at our departmental gallery at MIT, and invited audiences to engage in a form of work-shopping with us. We modeled the space on an activist headquarters, with room for contemplation and work alongside our own interventions.

How would you describe the differences between the Critical Broadcasting Lab and a program like Critical, Conceptual, and Curatorial Practices (CCCP) at Columbia University, which grants an advanced degree that provides tools for graduates to enter professional cura-torial practice?

I've thought about this question a lot. During *Agit Arch Outpost* we invited friends from CCCP to the gallery to talk about the materials we had produced and exhibited there. It was interesting for us to discuss the differences between a program like CCCP, which delivers a degree in curatorial practice but doesn't directly produce any hands-on curatorial work, and the Lab, which engages in producing statements and interventions into architectural discourse.

Maybe we could start a curatorial degree program through the Lab, but to me that's not the key point. The idea that we would somehow anoint or grant expertise in a particular way of curating architecture is less relevant than producing a set of artifacts and broadcasts that can enter into the discussion about architecture immediately and from a position that isn't compromised. If this kind of academic freedom can enable what we say but also allow what we say to then exit the confines of academia, that ability seems really valuable. Both CCCP and the Critical Broadcasting Lab carve out spaces within academia to think critically, *with* architecture and *about* architecture, and that is key at a time when it's clear that the field needs to undertake a hard-core inventory of itself and learn and absorb concerns that it has kept at a distance for far too long. In the context of an institution like MoMA, for example, the curatorial work must respond to other kinds of needs and interests, such as the number of visitors, whether the exhibit is profitable, and so on. So, even though the Lab's work is all done on a shoestring budget, there's real value in being able to determine exactly how and what we want to talk about.

> Could these differences in mission be described as a difference between the desire to intervene in a discourse directly through exhibitions and the desire to intervene in a discourse by producing future curators?

Our work has asked and enabled students to think in curatorial terms, but it may not have delivered something they can easily "cash in." The hope is that this sort of curatorial thinking will serve them as architects and citizens more broadly and prove valuable in producing conceptual and research work. For example, in the *Agit Arch Experiments* we produced something in just three weekends that gave us a lot of food for discussion, both as an exhibition and as a set of questions. But this probably isn't a model or training for how curatorial programming might work in a more conventional venue.

TENDING TO DISCOURSE

As someone who cares about and tends to pedagogy, I believe that having a program in which you can read, think, and produce in modalities other than professional design is valuable, regardless of what those students end up doing afterward or whether they happen to become certified as curators.

> Prior to establishing the Lab, you curated or co-curated several major exhibitions at venues around the world, including *OfficeUS* [the U.S. Pavilion at the Venice Biennale in 2014] and *Un/Fair Use* at the Center for Architecture in New York in 2015. Has working within the format of the Lab changed how you conceive of curatorial practice, particularly in terms of authorship?

The work that the Lab produces has fused the pedagogical project with a curatorial project for sure, but determining the correct ratio and the most effective way to organize the two projects is still a work in progress. Is the curatorial team in the Critical Broadcasting Lab me plus the research assistants? Where does authorship lie in that context? Many students have worked with me. Do I list them in perpetuity, in different contexts? Do I list them as Critical Broadcasting Lab?

ANA MILJAČKI

Are they? Were they? It's not necessarily clear yet
how authorship is defined.

What the structure of the Lab does allow
for is a kind of curatorial work to be produced from
within the pedagogical context and with direct
links to it. For example, our *Un/Fair Use* exhibition
(held a bit before I established the Lab, but already
a confirmation that the idea made sense) came out
of a research workshop. ○   The Lab's structure
also allows a set of questions that we think are
important to address without needing to have
external venues. We're able to explore simultaneously
a series of ideas *and* the curatorial or discursive
mechanisms by which one could develop them.
We've also been able to use the gallery of the MIT
School of Architecture + Planning as a kind of petri
dish, which is ideal in a way. My hope is that, once
we produce something that feels like it could have
a broader audience, we'll be able to bring it to an
external venue to develop an exhibition. However,
the curators of those venues aren't necessarily interested in operating in the same way we do, because
they also have their own curatorial programs and
approaches to consider. Publishers also have their
own agendas, but statements today can be sent out
into the world in many ways that don't flow through
traditional publication and exhibition formats.

TENDING TO DISCOURSE

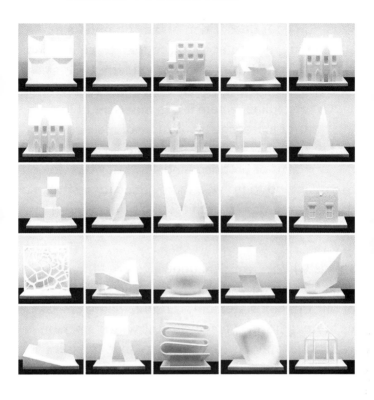

○
Installation views of models from the exhibition *Un/Fair Use*, September 18, 2015 to January 2, 2016, Center for Architecture, New York. Image courtesy of Ana Miljački.

> In your description of the Lab and its mission, you refer to "discourse" as something different from the catchall term that it's become in certain parts of the architectural discipline, where it can mean anything that increases the volume of messages; for example, through social media or other forms of broadcasting. In what ways do you intend to frame a more critical and strategic approach to architecture's disciplinary discourses, including curation?

This is where George Saunders's story "The Brain-dead Megaphone," which we describe at the start of our mission statement, is useful. Saunders asks us to imagine an average party at which a person with a megaphone—a technology that amplifies their statements—starts to exert an insidious social, aesthetic, and political influence on the partygoers. Whether they're aware of it or not, their priorities are gradually rewired—the sheer volume and repetition of his voice insinuates his messages into their conversations, their language, their attentions, and ultimately their reactions. Saunders's cautionary party is palpable today. He describes discourse simply as a set of exchanges, where distortion, simplification, and inflation diminish the quality of public discourse. The phenomenon he describes is part of the problem today.

Another person who provides an interesting perspective on the problems of contemporary discourse is Jodi Dean, who talks about "communicative capitalism," particularly with regard to social media. In the condition of communicative capitalism, people who in another version of capitalism would have been actively engaged politically are content solely to contribute to the flow of exchanges and are no longer able to ensure that their discursive participation in communication platforms has anything to do with actual political effect or affect. The two realms have become so separate that it's possible to have a robust, flowing discourse on one end that no longer has anything to do with actual political outcomes on the other. When you see the world framed in that way, it makes clear the importance of thinking critically about the nature of what we contribute to this existing flow of exchanges.

> How do you frame the "critical" project
> of the Lab in resisting this sort of neutering
> of discourse?

The objective for me is the production of more self-aware participants in the discipline and more

self-aware users of our collective architectural output.
If we were to conceptualize this work as being
about the production of discourse alone, as if that
were somehow an autonomous realm, then we
would absolutely be contributing to the problems
of communicative capitalism, where discourse is
severed from real political outcomes. I want to think
of discourse not in those terms but as something
that is productive of outcomes in all kinds of realms
in real life.

> Would you like to see a curatorial format
> like the Lab adopted in other academic
> institutions, or do you see this as something
> that could take place only within the
> particular institutional conditions of MIT?

Could something like the Critical Broadcasting Lab
be part of the larger model of architectural education? Yes. I think this already exists in many other
places, without being formed or figured in quite
the same way. What's interesting—and needs to be
discussed in this particular moment—are the kinds
of temporalities that course through any architecture school. Those temporalities include the idea
of a single architectural practice that endures for a
long time, and a historical understanding of practice

that's been around even longer, but also the personal lives of students and contemporary everyday politics. Those temporalities are all intertwined. Right now, certain urgencies occur on some of those registers that the Critical Broadcasting Lab enables, without having to push these concerns straight into the production of architecture. We're exploring what these might mean for the production of architecture without having to resolve them in an object, in a form, in a brick. For me, it's important that we become more sophisticated about articulating what the critical issues are, where they are, and how and when they intervene in the production of the architectural object.

> Architects often seek to oppose the realms of discourse and practice; for example, as a difference between the conceptions of architecture as a profession and as a discipline. What do you see as the boundaries, if any, between discourse and what we mean by architectural practice? How do you explore the limits of how "architecture" has been defined; for example, in the *Un/Fair Use* exhibition, where you explored the legal definition of architecture as it appears in disputes over copyright?

I don't draw a line between discourse and the discipline, certainly. I think they're the same thing. What I was referring to in *Un/Fair Use* was the clause in the copyright law that pertains to defining where architectural ideas reside. In earlier instances of copyright law, what was copyrighted were architectural drawings. They were understood as proxies or representatives for the architects. If you copied them, you were somehow infringing upon architects' copyright of those artifacts. The building itself wasn't copyrighted, even though the drawings obviously functioned to support the production of that building. The law now allows the idea of architecture to exist in the drawing, in the building, in a 3D model, and even in media we can't yet imagine. In that sense, I think this part of copyright law is smart. It's open-ended.

On the other hand, I think we're experiencing a moment where we can no longer understand the architectural object as an isolated object. That doesn't mean we lack expertise about the architectural object. It's just that suddenly the field of knowledge necessary for us to acknowledge, if not control and be experts at, is so much wider than form-making or tectonic assemblies. It includes anything from labor practices to material properties, sourcing, financing, and law. It's perhaps a conundrum for an architecture school to address, but for the discipline of architecture it may be an existential question. When you go to a place like São Paulo or Rotterdam, you encounter architecture in those contexts that is quite powerful in its own object-hood as architecture, as considered buildings. In the United States, though, we're not often surrounded with similar examples of such architecture. So you might worry about what happens to architecture if discourse is expanded to include broader topics, from how we work together to where architecture fits in the media flow.

That's all to say: I believe in architecture and also think architecture is discourse.

> Do you see any potential uses of social media as a curatorial space or as a territory that you can productively inhabit as part of the Lab's work? Or is falling back into the traps of communicative capitalism unavoidable?

I don't know whether I have a real or valuable answer here. We're trying to figure out social media at the Critical Broadcasting Lab. There's obviously something valuable about reaching the number of people that social media allows you to reach.

ANA MILJAČKI

It means that certain ways of broadcasting and even exhibiting are less valuable than others, or rather that at least the set of tools available is much wider than it has ever been. If you can make images or do TED talks that are seen by half a million people, why would you make a book? There's a kind of economy of attention that is now being transformed. At the Lab we don't know yet how to use the website versus Instagram versus Twitter. I look at my own profile on Instagram. I rarely post anything there, but I have an audience. We're still figuring out what that means. I worry about the erasure of context and information in the flow of social media, and I'm interested in gumming it all up, slowing it down. Instagram seems like an effective way to reach an audience, but I'm interested in including a short essay next to an image, something that might frame the image and its reception. It's hard to control how any information is actually taken in on the other end, but this may speak to my own levels of literacy with these broadcasting media rather than those audiences' sophistication in reading images.

> This conversation about social media as a discursive venue also seems very different now than it would have been even a few

years ago, as the cultural and political effects of social media have changed rapidly. Are there any other forms of broadcasting in the digital realm that you think have been more critical; for example, in slowing down or changing the rhythms of disciplinary discourse?

The landscape of digital and social media is constantly transforming. I know about TikTok and Snapchat, but have never used them and still have a Facebook account. That tells you where I'm stuck. So I can say less about the fast end of things, but I do think certain formats have been successful in slowing down the realm of digital dissemination. For me, the most successful ones right now are *The Avery Review* and *e-flux*, which are highly edited, extremely thought-out online collections of very labored texts. Access is easy, but the messages are not fast.

○
Dinner party (top) and Balls for All (bottom), events held as part of the
exhibition *Sharing Trainers*, September 10 to December 9, 2019, 12th
International Architecture Biennale of São Paulo, São Paulo.
Images courtesy of the Critical Broadcasting Lab.

Many of the Lab's curatorial projects engage with the idea of the collective and particularly with the possibilities for producing a kind of collective out of the audiences for the exhibition. This was the case in *Sharing Trainers*, the Lab's exhibition at the São Paulo Architecture Biennale in 2019, where the Lab exhibited a series of dinner-party objects that required various conditions of codependence on the part of their users. Can you speak more to this desire to explore forms of collectivity and care through curation?

The idea of *Sharing Trainers* was that our work could help in developing capacities and tolerances necessary for operating in a collective. ○ But care is a bigger thing. Collectives require care in very specific ways. For instance, who gets to speak? How much do they speak? Are you aware of the roles that people are given? Et cetera. There are various ways to care for a collective. But the notions of care and maintenance are different from the topic of the collective, even though they intersect in our piece. Certainly in the São Paulo project we injected some value that was collective. That's the most humorous of the pieces we created and the most lighthearted in response to our thoughts about the collective.

Shannon Mattern had a great piece in *Places Journal* on maintenance and care that addressed the topic from a variety of angles. It's a well-known feminist proposition that maintaining and caring—whether of the home, children, or a pedagogical institution—are forms of labor that aren't generally acknowledged as labor. An extension of that idea is that to study care is itself a form of care. We now need to discuss and elevate the things that are not tangible or heroic or that the discipline has not valued in the labor of care. This is what Mierle Laderman Ukeles described in 1969 in her "Maintenance Art Manifesto" as the issue of maintenance versus development: Who's going to pick up the trash after the revolution?

> How does this interest in collectivity and care relate to your "other" academic work as a historian of intersections between architecture and politics and, particularly, the role of individuals and collectives under socialist political systems?

I've studied the way architects operated under socialism in the Eastern European context specifically.

What you find when you study socialist regimes is that, while power structures were pronouncing socialism's arrival, its values and methods, while they were summoning socialism into existence, at every level one also finds active, local interpretations of the project of socialism. Both out of fear and out of solidarity, architects were deeply engaged in this complex dance of interpretation. Sometimes questions would arise about whether they had interpreted correctly (failure to do so could be costly), but in the final instance they operated on their own, at their desks, and from some form of private optimism that's necessary for the production of architecture. In both the Czechoslovak and Yugoslavian contexts there was also lots of support for valuing the collective.

I think this is a question our generation (broadly speaking) will have to ponder: the idea that our future is radically collective, or it isn't at all.

How we frame that question is going to be important. For *Sharing Trainers* we attempted to set it at the level of individuals engaging with our devices, as trainers for collective social practices such as sitting and eating together—feeding one another. The dinner party ended with a game that participants had to play communally called Balls for All, which we based on the tenets of Yugoslavian self-management. The game was initially produced by students in the Collective Architecture Studio offered by the Critical Broadcasting Lab.

An important aspect of the model of self-management in Yugoslavia is that, despite its various issues and problems in practice, the means of production and the means of living were socially owned, which is very different from run-of-the-mill state socialism where the state owns the means of production and distributes them together with the rules of operation. In a self-management model, whether an enterprise or units of living, stake-holders determine their faith. In the studio—and at the Critical Broadcasting Lab more generally—we thought it was important to both question and cultivate this model; at least that's how Balls for All and *Sharing Trainers* were meant.

> You mentioned humor and levity as tools you used to engage with audiences in São Paulo. Can these also be curatorial tools for building this kind of collective through the space of an exhibition?

In some cases we can (and did) use humor success-fully, but in others it might not be helpful. It very much depends on what is at stake in each project.

Communication through humor can invite delight and laughter. In the *Sharing Trainers* exhibition people quickly understood what was being asked of them. I found it fun and effective and would love to revisit that mode of address in future work. It's not only about engaging and delighting the audience, though, but also about promoting self-awareness of the positions we, ourselves, take. Yes, we do serious research, and we can talk about these issues in serious ways, but if we take ourselves too seriously, then ultimately we don't have an understanding of our own participation in that flow of discourse. I'm glad you noticed it, as it's not equally present in all of the work. The São Paulo project was a pleasure to work on because it felt like the narrative about the collective could be transmitted through a fun exhibition. But such a set of statements can also easily get lost in the era of communicative capitalism—"We've all enjoyed it, and now it's done." It's important to find ways to push back on the quickness with which information is consumed. And sometimes an exhibition will deliberately demand more laborious modes of engagement.

Can the exhibition also become a political outpost?

ANA MILJAČKI

That was the idea with the *Agit Arch Experiments*, a series of micro exhibitions that sought to instigate discussion and to critique and probe architectural discourse. ○   Each of the smaller entries also allowed us to test out a few ideas about address and posture. How do we engage an audience beyond the general (and often quick and dismissive) survey of what's presented? And if one could engage the material as an equal, as a comrade—that's again a term used by Jodi Dean—then you have an audience that's likely to care about the material in a particular way, and the mode of address may come out of that understanding or may invite the desired sentiment in turn.

Another project that started from our *Agit Arch* workshops and that we continued to develop afterward was called The Shape of Freedom. It started from looking at free-trade maps and how they operate as a kind of legal document. Students produced a series of maps—Free Trade, Free Play (on sites where gambling is allowed in the United States), Free Blank (a map of all of the U.S. military sites that are blanked out on Google Maps), Free Range (national parks), Free Love (dealing with sodomy laws across the country). Throughout the workshop we produced a series of outcomes based on the questions we were posing through

○
Installation view of the exhibition *Play Room*, February 14 to March 6, 2020, Keller Gallery, MIT, Cambridge.
Image courtesy of the Critical Broadcasting Lab.

the framework of "free." We ultimately produced an exhibition that we thought of as a political outpost where we could continue to do work on the topics we had started but also where we could engage and address our audience as comrades who come to the site and join us in producing knowledge and critical thought.

THE POLITICS OF THE ARCHIVE

An interesting through line in your work both before and after the Lab is the use of curatorial formats to build up an archive. For example, for *OfficeUS* you produced the Repository, an archive of more than 675 buildings designed by 169 U.S. architecture offices. The Repository lined the walls of the U.S. Pavilion in Venice as a kind of library for the office "partners" who were working out of the pavilion. Or in *Un/Fair Use*, for which you created a time line of court cases and other historical events that dealt with issues of appropriation and copyright in architecture. How do you see the role of the archive in these exhibitions?

Though they are many other things as well, both the *OfficeUS* and *Un/Fair Use* rely on a specific curatorial act that's available to historians, a specific kind of resetting of the table. ○   It's a gesture that communicates something like: this is the field we must look at. It's a deliberate flattening of sorts, a resetting of the framework, which ensures estrangement from the view we've become comfortable with, or from the canon, in order to figure out anew how to compare and measure things that haven't been compared before. On what terms are

○
Installation view of the OfficeUS Repository, part of the exhibition
OfficeUS, June 7 to November 23, 2014, U.S. Pavilion, Venice Architecture
Biennale, Venice, Italy.
Image courtesy of Ana Miljački.

they going to be comparable from now on? That's important. I'm not sure I would call it an archive in every case, but I do think it's a kind of a gesture of reproducing the boundaries of the field in a way that allows things to be asked of it anew.

> Thinking about your idea of participating as a comrade, would you also say that the space of the *OfficeUS* exhibition and the Repository could be read as inviting a more capitalist mode of participation, whether for the office partners or for visitors to the U.S. Pavilion?

The hope with *OfficeUS* was that the partners in the office would be the ones engaging the archive, our Repository, in true depth and adopting particular positions toward it. And then that the audience would engage the partners (who participated in the exhibit) and thereby the depth of their individual critique of the material: a historical record of U.S. contributions to global architectural thought over the past one hundred years. The idea was that one would momentarily become a part of that team and access the particular roads that the partners had begun to take. *OfficeUS*, or at least the Repository, was also about engaging the researcher audience.

It was about addressing the subject of the exhibition as someone capable of engaging the depth of information along with the partners, on their own or out of curiosity about what was going on there.

> How have you engaged with this notion of the exhibition creating an archive in your more recent work?

A more recent project of the Lab that deals with the archive is titled *I Would Prefer Not To*. The idea behind this project is that there are certain things that architects decide, ethical decisions that we make, which tend not to leave traces. Because of this, they're difficult to research and don't easily become part of the discussion. Putting these decisions on the record is the key point of the project.

The project has two chapters. One is about deciding not to take a fellow architect to court on intellectual property charges. The other is about deciding not to take on a particular design commission, either a building type or a specific commission. We ran these as a series of Skype interviews. The idea was to talk to as many architects as we could to produce an open-ended archive that would start as an exhibition, and that would then become available to others.

THE POLITICS OF THE ARCHIVE

What would this database or archive look like beyond the exhibition? Would it be an interface or something closer to a social media platform?

We worked on that issue. We had to decide whether an exhibition made sense given the material we had. We thought it could exist as an infinite archive to which could be added an infinite number of interviews with architects—all living somewhere online. We asked the MIT library whether it could host something like this, because then it would be much more of a resource than a celebration of the information. But the MIT library isn't currently equipped to host this kind of archive. It's an interesting question for the Lab to continue pursuing, because the whole point of this particular oral history project is that this kind of decision-making process—preferring not to take on a project for various reasons—ought to be available for us to discuss. If we manage to put some of that on the record, we then need to open it up for discussion. But we're not there yet.

You're talking about a desire to record the negative, the absent, or the ephemeral discussions that lead to not taking a project.

> This also seems like a feminist mode of practice, in the sense of narrating the absence, producing the absence as a presence.

Yes. This is where Ananya Roy's notion of an "innocent modernity" is important. The idea that the discipline has operated through erasure and through making some things simply not part of the discussion. The discipline reproduces itself by not engaging or acknowledging certain kinds of narratives that are part of it. So how do you allow some of those erased narratives to become more central than they've been or to return with some pushback?

> What do you see as the connection between the idea of the archive, the creation of discourse, and this preservation of historical memory?

Historical memory is an important element, and in the contemporary moment it's easy to lose or distort it amid our various ways of communicating and broadcasting all kinds of positions, including those that might be understood as forms of the cultural memory of historical events. Croatian philosopher Boris Buden critiques the fact that historical memory is transforming into cultural memory (in post-socialist transitions). I, on the other hand, think that the only way to recover historical memory is to restage it in cultural terms and to have a set of characters experience it as their own, preferably through collective experience. In many of the projects undertaken by the Critical Broadcasting Lab and in the work of *OfficeUS*, it's been important to tap into historical knowledge and determine how to re-perform it for an audience, or with an audience, so that such knowledge can become active in the decisions being made in the present—or soon to be made in the future.

Ana Miljački is Associate Professor of Architecture at the Massachusetts Institute of Technology, where she directs the Critical Broadcasting Lab. This conversation took place in Houston in November 2019.

ANN
LUI

CURATING
COLLECTIVE
SPACE

ANN LUI

What are the relationships between your work as a curator and your work as a practicing designer? What are your shared concerns or methods of connection between these two ways of working?

Creating platforms is important in both my curatorial projects and in my design work. In our work at Future Firm, we tend to work with clients or on self-initiated projects that deal with collectivity of different kinds. Curating and editing is also about creating collective space—physical space, as well as time, money, and visibility—for others to do their own work and share it with a broader audience. In architectural practice, I find myself collaborating with folks who share a similar point of view. I think this is the same case for architecture and design. My friend and client Eric Williams, for example, has cultivated and elevated the work of designers, musicians, and artists of color in his store the Silver Room in Chicago's South Side. When we collaborate, our approach to design, construction, and operation of a project reflects those efforts. It's not lost on me that Eric's platform-building mentality is why he took a risk on me as a relatively unproven architect.

In that way, building platforms for others, in both my curatorial work and my design practice, is personal. My own career has directly benefited from the efforts of people who at some time or another believed I had something interesting to say. Now I feel it's important to continue that momentum. It's also selfish, since I find it pleasurable to advance conversations in architecture that I personally find interesting. Exhibition and editorial work gives me a way to engage with ideas that I don't engage through professional practice, and vice versa. Practice can have a very narrowing effect on my worldview. It's easy to get bogged down in budgets, schedules, and the many challenges of trying to get things built in the world. Similarly, editorial and curatorial work can also be narrowing, but in another way, divorced from the urgency and stakes of non-architects doing business and trying to live in the complex messiness of cities. I think it's important to let those two points of view balance each other.

Are there lessons learned in the making of exhibitions that you've applied specifically to your architectural practice, or vice versa? How do the two modes of working inform each other?

ANN LUI

The approaches necessary for the two roles are very similar. I found that the skill sets needed for much of the curatorial work for *Dimensions of Citizenship*, the exhibition at the 2018 U.S. Pavilion at the Venice Architecture Biennale, were closely aligned with those needed for practice. ○   The biggest challenge in both curatorial and professional practice is negotiating divergent voices to produce an outcome that is more than the sum of its parts. The U.S. Pavilion had many stakeholders, each interested in having the project speak to their interests, and those visions had to be negotiated through many levels of review, from city to biennale to donor. Broadly, that is the same work as professional practice. The way the plumber sees a building is entirely different from the way the framer does, or the city's plan reviewer, or a bank approving construction payments. Ultimately, you need to bring everyone on board with a compelling "big idea" and also be able to further the priorities in the project that are significant to individual stakeholders. Of course, sometimes the job of the architect and curator is to recognize when those priorities are fundamentally at odds, and then the work is to set boundaries rather than to do translation.

In both types of practice, I've found it's important to leave room for people to surprise you.

○
In Plain Sight, Diller Scofidio + Renfro, Laura Kurgan, Robert Gerard
Pietrusko, with the Columbia Center for Spatial Research (top).
Installation view of the exhibition *Dimensions of Citizenship*, as part of
the 2018 U.S. Pavilion at the Venice Architecture Biennale (bottom).
Photographs by Tom Harris.
Images courtesy of the School of the Art Institute of Chicago and the
University of Chicago.

ANN LUI

I learned this from Mimi Zeiger, whose approach toward curating is a model for me. During *Dimensions of Citizenship* she often reminded me not to try to take too much control. From an architect's point of view, I was often frustrated by the lack of detail we received from participants about commissioned works during the planning process. But the works, once they emerged, surprised us in wonderful ways. I've since learned that clients and builders are collaborators and can surprise you in a good way if you leave space for it.

> Of course, we still debate what can be called curation or who can be called a curator. In recent years, these terms have become so expansive that almost anyone can be talked about as a curator, whether it's a curator of a menu, a conversation, or an exhibition. This differs from more specifically art-historical or institutional definitions of curatorial practice as a discipline. Do you have a position on these different definitions of the term curator?

I don't like gatekeeping. I'll never tell somebody they're not an architect if they want to say, "I'm an architect of my dinner plate." I'm not harmed by other people thinking about the work we do as a metaphor for the way they want to work or as a way of sparking different parts of their brain. Nonetheless, I want to acknowledge that the kind of ad hoc curating I do differs in major ways from the curatorial work of those who have spent a lifetime dedicated to the discipline of curating, as you described.

For me, the first battle in my practice was for the title of "architect," and that title is sometimes still not conceded to me despite the fact that I'm licensed and I build. People have referred to me as somebody who does "soft skills" work, such as curatorial work or community engagement. The folks who make that mistake also perceive soft skills as "lesser than," which is itself a form of ignorance.

I'm interested in this tension between valuing disciplinary expertise and expanding the boundaries of the discipline within architectural practice. On the one hand, I believe the built environment has always been the result of co-authored, multidisciplinary efforts. On the other hand, these days the importance of being licensed, insured, and executing technically proficient work for my clients does dominate my way of thinking. If you don't know anything about insulation, you don't have any business designing an exterior wall. First and foremost, a building project must be safe, structurally sound, and not leak. However, we should also expect more out of architecture. Depth of knowledge is important, but also breadth of experimentation, and those things shouldn't preclude each other but can exist in dialectical engagement.

> In your essay "Toward an Office of the Public Architect," you propose a new model of design practice to address public needs that can't adequately be addressed through the conventional architectural office. Can you talk about expanding the definition of the architect, especially considering your body of work, which navigates between architectural practice, curatorial work, and research and writing?

My essay in *Log*, "Toward an Office of the Public Architect," is an effort to expand the definition of the architect. It asks: If you're entitled to a public defender when you're accused of a crime and you can't afford an attorney, shouldn't you also be entitled to a public architect when you're issued a building violation that you may not have the means to address? I was trained as an architect in a very traditional way. After a five-year undergraduate degree, I then worked at SOM doing tall towers and corporate headquarters buildings. However, at SOM I always felt something was missing. I went back to school for a graduate degree in history, theory, and criticism, and colleagues there brought me over to the "dark side," where we understand architecture as part of larger sociocultural contexts rather than solely as a product for profit. The way most architects practice professionally is limited, yet those limitations provide a certain agency by enforcing a zone of professional expertise and responsibility. In my *Log* essay, I quote Ivan Illich, who argues that professions set the requirements for the things that only they can do. That's very much the case for architects. Architects were part of establishing the legal authority of building codes that dictate that only architects can be responsible for implementing them.

The Office of the Public Architect is design driven. It uses fiction and speculation as tools to imagine how a new kind of practice might manifest spatially. When we created the image of the Office of the Public Architect for the 2017 exhibition at the Chicago Architecture Foundation that led to the essay, we were trying to think about how to make something boring and bureaucratic into something emotionally compelling. The image we produced for the exhibition is kind of magical and surreal, showing an architect figure in a literal cyclone of paperwork. We were thinking of the moment in the first Harry Potter movie where ten-year-old Harry goes to the wand shop and finally holds the magic wand he was destined for—there's a sudden glow as objects around him begin to rise into the air. We wanted to evoke that feeling of a pivotal moment of change, about the work we each may be destined in one way or another to do, but for the Department of Buildings, which in real life is a beige office in Chicago's City Hall with crappy laminated desks and peeling paint.

INCORPORATING OTHERS

You mentioned stakeholders as a driving force in both your curatorial work and your design practice. How has your work been affected by the evolving set of collaborators you've worked with—from your first curatorial project, *Circus for Construction*, to the Night Gallery in Chicago, to the U.S. Pavilion at the Venice Biennale?

No architectural project of scale, whether a building or an exhibition, is ever produced in isolation. That part of exhibition-making has been clear to me since the beginning, even with self-initiated, low-budget efforts like *Circus for Construction* or the Night Gallery. Any pavilion in Venice is the result of the collaboration of an extraordinary number of people, acknowledged or not, even though a kind of star system surrounds the commissioned participants and the curators. *Dimensions of Citizenship* was executed in large part by local builders, tradespeople, and cultural workers in administration, such as grant writers, project managers, and so on.

How can we bring the stakeholders of a project like the U.S. Pavilion to community-led projects or to independent, off-the-beaten-path work? What was amazing to me about the U.S. Pavilion was the scale of funding that was mobilized in a relatively short period of time. In some cases, we worked with philanthropists or institutions with records of support for research in specific areas—say, sustainability and ecology. However, other funders seemed open to hearing from curators and designers about what topics should be of urgent concern. Can curatorial work, understood as a process of translation and framing, be used to redirect funding and opportunity toward individuals and communities that aren't receiving the same kind of visibility? I've been wondering how I can connect my curatorial work to the pro bono work I've been doing as a practitioner—using the same tools of making things legible, meaningful, and understandable to different audiences?

> Could you describe your pro bono work
> in more detail and the relationships
> you see between this work and your
> curatorial practice?

I'm currently working pro bono with community members in North Lawndale on the Central Park Theater in Chicago's West Side. The theater is "the mothership" of collaborations between movie palace developers Balaban & Katz and architects

Rapp & Rapp. The church that owns the building has been unable to heat it for the past five years. For that, they really just need a furnace and some spiral ducts to stave off further damage, which costs nothing compared to what is regularly funded by major donors to the Venice Biennale. Can curatorial techniques be used to advocate for the significant historical value of this building, for its opportunity to function again as an arts and culture hub for the neighborhood? Can we organize tours? Can we have it photographed beautifully? Can we do a publication? Can those things give it the kind of sparkle and legibility that will make it interesting to the same kinds of donors who are interested in the U.S. Pavilion? We've made some progress on this front: the theater will be part of the Chicago Architecture Biennial 2021, so we'll see if that has the positive effect we imagine.

I've also been working over the last two years in collaboration with the Bluhm Legal Clinic at Northwestern University to support victims of a reverse mortgage scam. A fraudster stole ten million dollars from dozens of North Lawndale home-owners by telling them they were signing up for a city-sponsored repair program. Sometimes I contribute in my capacity as a traditional practitioner; for example, by evaluating the extent of a home's disrepair or using my role as a licensed professional to try to get calls returned. Right now, I'm working on a contribution to a website led by the team at Bluhm; it educates elderly homeowners about their legal rights and responsibilities, as well as home-owner and construction issues—what are common building violations, what can be solved by an architect versus a contractor, what are existing vetted resources, and so on. I see that work as curatorial, too, as it aims to translate general knowledge about buildings in a way that is legible and useful. It's also a mini-pilot for the Office of the Public Architect.

> You collaborated with historians Ana María León and Andrew Herscher and Heather Miller from the American Indian Center on the Settler Colonial City Project for the 2019 Chicago Architecture Biennial. How did you see the boundaries of your role as a de-signer when working in a collaboration with other curators or exhibitors?

What's interesting is that Ana María, Andrew, and Heather were commissioned as participants, but I feel as if they approached their involvement as building curators. Other participants produced work that could be placed in a room alongside work that was similar and relevant. Ana María and Andrew resisted that approach, instead proposing didactic physical signs throughout the Chicago Cultural Center that challenged one's understanding of the entire building. These signs shared research describing the building's siting, decor, construction, and materiality through the lens of a long history of both violence against Indigenous people and their resilience. Ana María, Andrew, and Heather engaged the building at a 1:1 scale and challenged visitors to understand it discursively. ○   In my opinion, the Settler Colonial City Project shaped the reading of all the other projects in the exhibition.

My role on that project was essentially as a technical designer. Architecture can act purely in support of others' efforts to change the built environment, and that's an important part of the work I do. Supporting people behind the scenes through technical means, through negotiations with different regulatory agencies, through the procurement and deployment of materials, can be both curatorial and architectural work if it enables others to make change at a different scale.

Curators think about the idea of audience in different ways. One your earliest collaborative projects, *Circus for Construction*—

ANN LUI

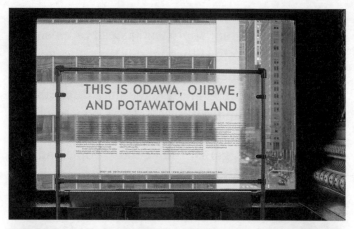

○
Settler Colonial City Project, *Decolonizing the Chicago Cultural Center*,
as part of the 2019 Chicago Architecture Biennial (top).
Circus for Construction, as part of WorldWide Storefront, a Storefront
for Art and Architecture, New York, project, 2014 to 2015 (bottom).
Photographs by Tom Harris.
Images courtesy of Future Firm.

a mobile exhibition space designed for the back of a flatbed truck—is very much both an architectural and a curatorial work, but it's also a project for audiences that are not necessarily typical in an institutional or museum setting. Who do you see as the audiences for your work?

With *Circus*, the idea of audience was almost flipped. ○　　Rather than the exhibition being a host to others, we were knocking on doors asking to be part of other people's worlds for a little bit. We were all students at the time, and in retrospect it was a form of curating driven by curiosity and a certain hunger for ways of doing architecture that might exist outside the academic bubble. We were consuming first, then amplifying. We weren't as discerning about having a certain kind of legibility for any specific audience. The actual audience often reflected our partners at local sites. When we were in Buffalo, for example, the folks who came to our events were the friends and colleagues of the people who hosted us. That group included academics, as well as a group of residents and builders who at the time were informally managing and activating Silo City, the complex of abandoned grain elevators where we held the exhibition.

ANN LUI

With *Dimensions of Citizenship*, we grappled with the question of audience because the audience for the Venice Architecture Biennale is so narrow. It's limited to the discipline's glitterati if you don't challenge it. We created CitizenSHIP, a series of events that roamed around the city, like *Circus for Construction*; it was led by our co-curator Niall Atkinson. It included a series of pop-up events with local organizations focused specifically on the impacts of tourism and definitions of citizenship in Venice. We later brought the exhibition back to Chicago, to a private gallery called Wrightwood 659, with varying levels of success. We also tried to expand that platform by having a strong internet presence. With our project Form N-X00, we asked people to submit an Instagram-scale work—an image and a text. We asked each participant to phone a friend; these friends would then expand the platform exponentially to people outside the curators' immediate circles.

I've always tried to be critical about which audiences are reached by an exhibition but also to recognize the limitations of exhibitions as a medium. The entire nine months of the Venice Biennale—the biggest architecture exhibition there is—probably has the numerical audience of one day of HGTV. We can't be too self-serious about our own impact.

INCORPORATING OTHERS

You talked about the idea of collectivity when you're designing and working with clients. Do you consider your curatorial work as a way of interfacing with a public or as work that creates a kind of collectivity? How does this relate to the idea of expanding the role of the architect?

One of the questions I struggle with is how to build trust. I've been working on a few projects in North Lawndale, a predominantly African American community in Chicago that is facing many of the impacts of systemic racism in the built environment. I'm an outsider to the neighborhood, and I practice there knowing that there's not necessarily a built-in trust for outsiders within the community. I've heard stories from residents in North Lawndale about architects showing up, even well-intentioned ones, with plans, ideas, and renderings that never materialize. I've also heard stories about architects and contractors who treat projects as disposable. At best they send their B teams; at worst, they fail to follow through with the project.

My colleague Paola Aguirre, who is a strong advocate for equity in planning and design, told me, "Just do what you say you're going to do." Curating was something I already knew how to do, and it offered a way of building trust by "doing what you say" faster than through traditional architecture projects. For example, we organized an event in collaboration with Principle Barbers in North Lawndale as part of our exhibition project The Night Gallery. Bobby Price, a resident who owns and runs the barbershop, thought of the event in the same way I think an architecture exhibition should work. When he was growing up, the neighborhood barbershop was a place where he saw all kinds of people, from congressional representatives to school kids, and there was a horizontality to the kinds of conversations that happened there. When he started his own barbershop, he wanted to create a space embodying that horizontality that could also be used for meetings and gatherings. He's hosted a series of curated events there, from performances to campaign events to film screenings.

We collaborated with Bobby on a version of Night Gallery, our public space video and film exhibition project. ○   Together we curated the work of West Side artist avery r. young and Chicago artist Ciera McKissick for an outdoor evening event. avery worked with the South Side Home Movie Project, an archival and research initiative that collects and maintains footage of the daily lives of African American Chicagoans from past decades.

○
Installation view of *Another Campo Marzio*, by Outpost Office, as part of
The Night Gallery, 2017 (top).
Conversation with Ciera Alyse McKissick and avery r. young, as part of
The Night Gallery in collaboration with South Side Home Movie Project at
Principle Barbers, 2020 (bottom).

It's footage that has been left out of most film archives. avery screened a film from the 1968 riots in North Lawndale and performed a live ekphrastic work that responded to the film through music. In the audience were people who had lived in North Lawndale for sixty years and remembered the riots. They recognized people and places in the film, which was projected on the side of the building. Also in attendance were members of the architecture community who, because of Chicago's segregation, had never been to the West Side before.

> Architecture can also provide an opportunity to build community. Even for architects and other stakeholders who seek to engage with community members, though, conventional models of practice often have difficulty engaging them substantively in the process. How would you compare the capacity of exhibitions to build community?

Architects should be thinking about how to share a way of seeing and understanding buildings with people who aren't trained in architecture. That's not the goal of all exhibitions and doesn't have to be. Many exhibitions are meant to communicate only to a specific subset of other architects and can be important for producing new disciplinary knowledge. However, exhibitions should have a role in exploring ways to read or understand buildings. One example is the Settler Colonial City Project. I believe that project resonates with so many people because it shares a new way of "reading" a building. It suggests that the materials of the building, the land on which it sits, and the ways in which the building codifies different histories all matter. If there's a way to think or talk about buildings in a different way that can be mediated by exhibitions, that seems to me to be an important potential.

> Many curators affiliated with institutions
> are tasked with positioning work within
> white-box constraints. How do you, as an
> independent curator or as a practicing
> architect, rethink the spatial constraints that
> other institutional actors are beholden to?

Perhaps other forms of curatorial practice might
have the freedom to ignore these dimensions of the
built environment—to treat spaces in abstraction
and expect the audience to suspend disbelief about
the context they're in and get lost in the work. But I
think the second you ask people to take on architectural space discursively, you're saying that drawings,
materials, and the ways in which things are built
have meaning. You have a burden to engage discursively the space you're in if that's the way you want
people to think about architectural practice. This
is a way of thinking, looking, and working that can
apply anywhere. All buildings, let's say, have both
fraught and wonderful histories.

Thinking about the Settler Colonial City
Project, I believe it will be difficult for anybody
doing an exhibition there afterward to treat
the Chicago Cultural Center as a white box. The
histories they foregrounded are now too loud,
and rightfully so. In *Dimensions of Citizenship*,

○
Thrival Geographies (In My Mind I See a Line), by Amanda Williams and
Andres L. Hernandez in collaboration with Shani Crowe. Photographs
by Tom Harris.
Images courtesy of the School of the Art Institute of Chicago and the
University of Chicago.

commissioned participants Amanda Williams,
Andres L. Hernandez, and Shani Crowe critically
engaged the neo-Jeffersonian architecture of the
U.S. Pavilion, which was built in the 1930s. Their
work in the courtyard of the pavilion, *Thrival
Geographies (In My Mind I See a Line)*, was an act
of resistance to the space around it. ○   When
you were inside the steel and woven structure they
built, you could look up into the sky and, in a
way, escape the world around you. It was important
for them, in speaking about histories of space-
making by Black women, to acknowledge the fact
that the U.S. Pavilion was built in the style of a
plantation building.

As of the summer of 2020, we've also seen
institutions that want to bring forward Black
artists, architects, and designers but don't want to
treat Black curators or cultural workers equally.
We've seen so many examples of the ways in which
institutions, because of old habits, fail their own
purported values. I believe there has to be a way for
institutions and individuals to be self-reflective and
self-critical, and that doing so always makes the
world around us richer, more interesting, and more
expansive. A design practice should also consider
its own practices suspect. There's always a way of
engaging buildings in both curating and practice

that is discursive, that resists the easier illusion of the white box. For example, making an architecture exhibition should mean that the architecture in which the exhibition takes place is also under scrutiny.

> Your proposal to create an Office of the Public Architect began as your firm's contribution to a 2017 exhibition, titled *Between States,* in which the vast majority of architects who participated showed more conventional design projects. Is this different mode of participation in exhibitions related to the size of Future Firm's design practice? What nimbleness does a smaller practice afford you in thinking across curatorial and architectural opportunities?

Between States was the second exhibition held at the Chicago Architecture Center (then Foundation) during the Chicago Architecture Biennial. It included all the big architecture firms, like SOM, AECOM, HDR, and Gensler. We were the smallest firm by far. At that point, Future Firm was just me and my partner, Craig Reschke. The next smallest firm in the exhibition had probably two hundred employees, while the largest had twenty thousand!

ANN LUI

The brief called for a realistic project that could have an impact. We knew that all the big firms were going to show large-scale mixed-use projects for programs like affordable housing, cultural hubs, and infrastructure.

As a tiny firm, how could we try to say that the tiny stuff also has an impact? That's where the idea of the Office of the Public Architect emerged. None of the other firms were going to be talking about building violations, which are largely considered unglamourous, poorly paid, thankless work for architects to address. However, you could argue that violations work might have the biggest positive impact on Chicago communities—by scale and number, if not by architects' fees. In an exhibition with very tight format limitations, where you get to show one image or one model, we tried to do something that responded differently from the other work presented. As an exhibition participant, I enjoy "biting the hand that feeds." It allows you to surprise people. This is different from how we work with clients, of course, where that way of working would be counterproductive to our shared goals.

Can you speak to the difference between the physical space of the exhibitions you've curated and the editorial and digital platforms that accompany and often exist beyond them?

Unlike buildings, which have indeterminate futures, most exhibitions have a definitive end date. But an exhibition should be the beginning of things, not the end. At the 2018 Venice Biennale, some of the national pavilions didn't approach curating as a tool for beginning a longer-term conversation. There was a trend in our year where architects produced installations that were mostly meant to be experienced in the moment and that seemed to be purposely apolitical. For me, to arrive in Venice with no interest in catalyzing conversation beyond the immediate physical experience, or to choose not to share the platform with other voices that might conflict with or challenge us as curators, would have felt like a squandered opportunity.

Dimensions of Citizenship didn't answer many of the questions we began with, though it answered other questions that we didn't expect. But what has been really rewarding is seeing the scholarly and research works have a ripple effect and continue on, whether into other exhibitions, as references in student work, or as citations that other scholars or designers are building upon.

> How did you approach the installation of the seven projects in *Dimensions of Citizenship* in a way that responded to the specific temporality of the Biennale and its audience while also setting up the projects for a life beyond the exhibition?

Mimi Zeiger and I wanted the exhibition to be easily legible in a literal way. We wanted both the people who spend hours with an exhibition and the people who run through it in thirty seconds (a common speed at which people experience the Biennale) to glean something from it. Robert Somol says that architecture can either be "What? Wow!" or "Wow! What?" One can either be impressed and then confused, or confused and then impressed. Ideally, the strongest work leaves you impressed and then impressed; it has both a short-term legibility and a long-term legibility. In *Dimensions of Citizenship*, the work on display in the U.S. Pavilion was organized using seven scales, from the citizen to the cosmos. If you were to walk through, you would proceed telescopically from the human scale upward through the scales of the civic, the regional, the national, the global, the networked, and the cosmic. The exhibition was also circular, so a sense of continuity remained.

The moments we were most excited about in the space were those in which you might see different resonances across scales. For example, mapping and cartographic projects physically bookended the pavilion at different scales: by Teddy Cruz and Fonna Forman at the scale of the nation and by DS+R, Laura Kurgan, and Robert Gerard Pietrusko at the global scale. Both of these projects questioned the ways in which maps do or do not reflect the lived experience of folks on the ground, through very different approaches and levels of granularity. ○ The exhibition also included a series of one-to-one artifacts—stones, asteroids, and porous concrete blocks—that together talked about how rocks and material objects might have agency in constructing citizenship at different scales. We used visual strategies to try to give a quick impression but also to let visitors learn more if they stayed with any of the works for a long time. Works were often paired with films that provided more depth. If a visitor had time, for example, they could easily spend two hours with Keller Easterling and MANY's project, reading all the descriptions in the app and imagining all the possible combinations,

Mexus: A Geography of Interdependence, by Estudio Teddy Cruz + Fonna Forman. Photographs by Tom Harris.
Images courtesy of the School of the Art Institute of Chicago and the University of Chicago.

and it still wouldn't be enough. But they could also just walk by it and quickly understand the idea of a Tinder-like app for connecting individuals and groups in ways that elude national boundaries or restrictions.

Many of the projects also included longer-term strategies that extended beyond the Biennale. SCAPE's project, *Ecological Citizens*, contained marsh rebuilding units that went into the Venetian lagoon after the Biennale closed and formed part of a remediation strategy at a specific site nearby.

> In the introductory essay for *Dimensions of Citizenship*, you framed the exhibition as speaking to two temporalities: to the direct urgency of issues of citizenship in the political context of 2018, but also to the broader questions of community and belonging that transcend those urgencies and are oriented toward futures.

It's important for us to situate things in multiple time frames. We wrote the proposal for *Dimensions of Citizenship* in the months between Donald Trump's election and inauguration. Our work was partially funded by the State Department under the Trump administration, and it was important for us to recognize and resist our own complicity through the staging of the exhibition. For us, trying to acknowledge this tension was essential, even if the projects didn't solve or untangle it completely. During the Black Lives Matter protests in the summer of 2020, it was more evident than ever to me that issues that seemed particularly visible or cruel under the Trump administration were battles people have been fighting for a long time across many governmental and political contexts. Those battles continue and are agnostic to any specific administration in certain respects, which is to say that a defining characteristic of both racism and xenophobia is their durability as ideologies. Mimi and I wanted *Dimensions of Citizenship* to acknowledge that citizenship, and questions of belonging, were both newly and forever urgent. Beyond this, we also wanted to look forward through speculation. One of our commissioned participants, Andres L. Hernandez, connected us with a text by author and Afrofuturist Samuel Delany that calls on us to produce images of tomorrow—for better and worse—so we might know how to get there, before it arrives on its own. We challenged all of the works to balance these ways of engaging with time, and I think they each did so in their own ways.

ON TEMPORALITY AND MODALITY

Looking back, how do you situate the aspects of *Dimensions of Citizenship* that could be read as more temporally specific to that moment, like the interrogation of the U.S.-Mexico border wall, since many of the broader questions about citizenship, belonging, and our commitments to one another as individuals and as communities persist today?

The border wall was mostly addressed in Estudio Teddy Cruz + Fonna Forman's work. They have been working in Tijuana and San Diego for a long time, and the kinds of projects they presented in Venice contribute to a longer project that both preceded the Trump administration's attempts to build the wall and will continue beyond it. The work made visible many aspects of the border that are cruel, violent, or just nonsensical, and some of which were part of Trump's construction campaign. Beyond this, the work mapped interconnected watersheds as a socio-ecological terrain that has shaped how the border region evolved and will continue to be shaped. In this way, their work in *Dimensions of Citizenship* will continue to remain relevant, though I'm sure the bigger project—which is grounded in local communities at the border—will also continue to evolve.

I would say the same about Amanda Williams, Andres L. Hernandez, and Shani Crowe's work, which carried the mantra "Black woman space matters." Their work impacted me personally by challenging me to change my point of view during our production of the exhibition. At the time, I was so grateful for the work's generosity, which manifested in the breadth of its vision and catalyzed that personal process for me. This year, during the nationwide reckonings with police brutality and the resurgence of violence against Asian Americans, their work, *Thrival Geographies*—with its emphasis on transcendence through survival—has even more resonance for me than it did before.

Some formats of the exhibition may become dated, for sure. Tinder, which was the basis for Keller Easterling and MANY's project, will probably seem absurdly out of date in two years as an example of an app, but that's the nature of the medium. Other projects will be measured by their impact at one-to-one scale. A part of Studio Gang's project in Memphis is now under construction in collaboration with SCAPE. Will it be embraced or challenged? Like all public spaces, it will likely be an unexpected mixture of both. Ultimately, I hope our curation didn't center the political context of 2018 too much, which would have made the works less accessible beyond that time. Some of the texts in the catalog helped expand the work beyond the exhibition and uncovered histories or introduced possible futures that made them relevant beyond that particular moment.

> If the experience of an exhibition is grounded in a moment in time, how do you engage a sense of timelessness through the artifacts?

We can read all exhibitions as indexing their moment, place, and authorship, whether they do so consciously or not. That's an analytical tool that we have at our disposal as people who are interested in curating. I don't think anything can avoid being in the world in which it is made, even if it tries. I hope we can remember to struggle with the specific moment of an exhibition, with all its material and geographical specificity. That struggle is something that can be built into an exhibition, rather than work that is only done analytically by third parties afterward.

Ann Lui is a registered architect and founding principal of Chicago-based Future Firm. This conversation took place via Zoom in December 2020.

APPENDIX

INDEX

INDEX

INDEX

INDEX

INDEX

EXHIBITIONS 1889–2015

Exposition Universelle (1889)
Paris
Modern Architecture: International Exhibition (1932)
The Museum of Modern Art, New York
House in the Museum Garden (1949)
The Museum of Modern Art, New York
Good Design (1950–1951)
The Museum of Modern Art, New York
Art in Daily Life: Well-Designed Objects Made in Mexico (1952)
Palacio de Bellas Artes, Mexico City
This Is Tomorrow (1956)
Whitechapel Art Gallery, London
Buildings for Business and Government (1957)
The Museum of Modern Art, New York
Expo '58, Brussels World's Fair (1958)
Brussels
Expo '70, Osaka World's Fair (1970)
Osaka
Information (1970)
The Museum of Modern Art, New York
Italy: The New Domestic Landscape (1972)
The Museum of Modern Art, New York
Instant Malaysia (1973)
Commonwealth Institute, London
MAN transFORMS (1976)
Cooper Hewitt National Museum of Design, New York
Transformations in Modern Architecture (1979)
The Museum of Modern Art, New York
Sensation (1997)
Royal Academy of Arts, London
Humble Masterpieces (2004)
The Museum of Modern Art, New York
Massive Change (2005)
Vancouver Art Gallery
Actions: What You Can Do With the City (2008–2009)
Canadian Centre for Architecture, Montreal
Some Ideas on Living in London and Tokyo (2008)
Canadian Centre for Architecture, Montreal
404 ERROR: The object is not online (2010–2011)
Canadian Centre for Architecture, Montreal
Journeys: How Travelling Fruit, Ideas and Buildings Rearrange Our Environment (2010)
Canadian Centre for Architecture, Montreal
Architecture in Uniform (2011),
Canadian Centre for Architecture, Montreal
Bertrand Goldberg: Architecture of Invention (2011–2012)
Art Institute of Chicago
Imperfect Health: The Medicalization of Architecture (2011)
Canadian Centre for Architecture, Montreal
Yung Ho Chang and FCJZ: Material-ism (2012)
UCCA, Beijing
Archaeology of the Digital (2013)
Canadian Centre for Architecture, Montreal
Building M+: The Museum and Architecture Collection (2014)
ArtisTree, Hong Kong
Mobile M+: NEONSIGNS.HK (2014)
Mobile M+, Hong Kong
OfficeUS (2014)
U.S. Pavilion, Venice Architecture Biennale
Archivo Italia (2015–2016)

EXHIBITIONS DISCUSSED

*Ambiguous Standards Institute: An
Institute within an Institute* (2021)
  Art Institute of Chicago
*Reconstructions: Architecture and
Blackness in America* (2021)
  The Museum of Modern Art,
  New York
*The Project of Independence: Archi-
tectures of Decolonization in South
Asia, 1947–1985* (2022)
  The Museum of Modern Art,
  New York

ACKNOWLEDGMENTS

A book of this kind is inevitably collaborative in nature, and it would not exist without the dedicated work of everyone involved.

First, we thank the masterclass students whose intelligence and curiosity forms the foundation of this project: Gabriela Degetau, Claire Elestwani, Ana Escobar, Drake Flood, Kohen Hudson, Shree Kale, Jiaye Li, Nicole Lide, Mitch Mackowiak, Jack Murphy, Aylin Nazli, Irene Nguyen, Kaede Polkinghorne, Matthew Ragazzo, Sheila Rodriguez, Samantha Schuermann, Esther Tang, Sonia Torralba, Nyx Valerdy, Jane Van Velden, Claire Wagner, Ashley Whitesides, and Tiffany Xu. The project also benefitted from our discussions in the "Exhibiting Space" seminar, for which we thank students Adesoji Adeseyoju, Kalyani Bhatt, Brendan Carr, Tristan Durham, Grace Ehmling, Ariana Flick, Drake Flood, Eugenia Forgang, Rahma Hassan, Matt Hewett, Shuo Jiang, Daniyal Latif, Richard Liu, Hélène de Mello, Shinji Miyajima, Jad Moghnieh, Hannah Montalvo, Irene Nguyen, Kenny Nguyen, Alexandra Oetzel, Kaede Polkinghorne, Neha Sahai, Alexander Salinas, Brenda Tijerina, and Gregorio Zavary.

A conversation is only as good as its participants. We are grateful for the contributions of the seven curators—Mario Ballesteros, Giovanna Borasi,

ACKNOWLEDGMENTS

Ann Lui, Ana Miljački, Zoë Ryan, Martino Stierli, and Shirley Surya—and thank them especially for their generosity in providing insight into the universe of their extraordinary work and for their willingness to engage in substantive discussions about that work.

Maria Nicanor, Roberto Tejada, Alison Weaver, and Sandra Zalman were important inter-locutors, as respondents to the public lectures. We would also like to thank Nisa Ari, Giovanna Borasi, Salomon Frausto, Ann Lui, Donald Mak, Mary McLeod, Noëmi Mollet, and Mimi Zeiger for their invaluable advice and critical suggestions as the project developed.

A Humanities Research Center masterclass at Rice University, as well as a seminar co-taught at the Gerald D. Hines College of Architecture and Design at the University of Houston and the Rice University School of Architecture, formed the foundation of this project. We thank Patricia Oliver, Sarah Whiting, and Farès el-Dadah for providing institutional support for this collective project. Thank you to Mary Leclère and Peter Gershon at the Core Program at the Glassell School of Art and to Alison Weaver at Rice's Moody Center for the Arts for allowing us to hold our events in their spaces, extending the public reach of these dialogues.